MW00905505

# DOWN TO THE SEA: discovering grandfather by following in his wake

JAMES WHITE

with James
McKay

For Billie, for Stuart and for the McKay and White families.
My thanks to M.G. Vassanji for his mentorship.

Figure 1            James McKay, RN

# CONTENTS

Excerpts from James McKay's diary written aboard HMS Lancaster between 1910 and 1912 are in Italics.

# CHAPTER 1: FINDING GRANDFATHER

My mother died after a short illness in 2000, one month short of her 91$^{st}$ birthday. She had been living alone in her London flat where she had lived with my father until he died in 1998. I sometimes think that she must have died disappointed, for she often said that she wanted to live to be a hundred, the world being such an exciting place. Immediately after getting the news of her death I went back to England from Canada where I have lived for forty years. After her funeral, my sisters sorted out the household effects while I took on the task of clearing out her desk and her files. Her desk, piled with old copies of the Times (which she was always intending to read or clip), stood in a corner of the dining room. She never had her own study. After clearing the stacks of newspapers I moved the contents of the drawers into the bedroom where her files were stored in a closet. I was able to sort through her material there without interference from the rest of the household.

My mother was a pack rat. I ploughed through piles of her lecture notes and reports from long ago. She had kept copies of correspondence and job interviews. I was daunted by the task as I separated the "keep" files from the "garbage" files. After labouring with this task for about two hours I discovered a buff-coloured file labeled "DIARY." I was astonished; I never knew my mother kept a diary. I was

1

excited too; perhaps this would reveal her secret thoughts—my mother was a reserved person, who kept most of her feelings to herself. Unfortunately the file did not contain her diary. But there was a stack of photocopies of handwritten original pages. It was far too neat to be mother's scrawl. The handwriting flowed and was even-spaced. This was her father James McKay's diary.

The first page was entitled: **HMS Lancaster, 1910 to 1912.** As I hastily flipped through the pages and read the odd excerpt, I realized that they were James McKay's account of his experiences during the commission of a Royal Navy cruiser, HMS Lancaster, in the Mediterranean. I vaguely remembered mother mentioning the original diary and brandishing it in my direction in the early 1980's, but I had very little interest in reading it then. Years later she told me that she had attempted to have it published without success, and finally presented it to the National Maritime Museum in Greenwich outside London. I was delighted to find that she had photocopied it, because family history had come to mean so much more to me as I grew older.

I sat on my parents' bedroom floor that morning, becoming more and more intrigued by the words of my grandfather– this man who had died 23 years before I was born and whose war citation and my first name were the only connections I had with him. During my childhood Mother did not talk much about her father. He had been killed in the "Great" War when she was four. I knew that he had been a Warrant Officer in the Royal Navy and that he and my grandmother were born and raised in Scotland.

The diary begins with a poem:

2

*Oh, lang may Scotia's sturdy sons*

*In joy and mirth foregather*

*To sing the praises o' their home,*

*The land of snuff and heather.*

*The land o' porritch, brose, and kail,*

*O' puddin's fair and dusky,*

*The hame o' haggis, tripe & spuds,*

*And the medicine ca'd whisky.*

*The land o' Dukes, saut fish & flukes,*

*The lanky leggit partan*

*The haunts o' potted head & jam*

*O' marmalade and tartan.*

*Oh, Scotland mine, I'll surely dine,*

*When back to thee I wander*

*On brose or kail and Younger's ale,*

*To quench my thirst and hunger.*

I was taken with his simplistic but ardent love of Scotland. Was he feeling homesick when he wrote it? Did he expect not to return for a long time? As it turned out, he never saw Scotland again. My mother had been proud of her Scottish heritage in our South African and English surroundings; she retained a refined Scottish accent to the end of her life and served us haggis with neeps (turnips) and tatties (mashed potatoes) on Robbie Burns' birthday. She regarded Hogmanay (New Year's Eve festivities) as just as important as Christmas. Her regard for things Scottish rubbed off on me, beginning with the gift of a kilt by my favourite Scots uncle, Colin, when I was ten. I loved the way it swished as I walked. I endured some ribald comments from my school mates but I wore it with pride until I outgrew it

Following the poem, grandfather describes his preparations for a voyage round the Mediterranean which would mean his being away from his home, his wife and his growing family for two and a half years:

*I was hurriedly recalled from my quiet little job of initiating 2nd class stokers on H.M.S. Acheron (*a training vessel*) into the mechanical duties which are required of them below decks in the H. M. Navy. On entering the barracks I was told to hold myself in readiness to commission the Lancaster for the Mediterranean and in the meantime to muster before the doctor. After the usual eyesight test etc; I was told to attend next morning at 9 o'clock to see the dentist. I had several qualms before entering his sanctum as I happened to be the unfortunate possessor of a few decaying molars and he held a great reputation for being zealous in the matter of ridding people of undesirable grinders. He passed me however and I was now ready to avail myself of the ten*

4

*days leave which is granted on these occasions to enable one to say goodbye to friends and relations.*

*The ten days passed all too quickly and Saturday the 28th of May found me along with the ship's company mustered once more before the doctor in case, I suppose, we had enjoyed ourselves not wisely but too well on our ten days. This ordeal over we were free to go ashore for the weekend (bar those detained for duty). I had my mind made up to go and have a look round Chatham, probably the last opportunity for two years, and accordingly pushed off after seeing my chest packed and all my belongings in order.*

As I read these passages I felt a certain thrill. I couldn't help feeling that I was in communion with a part of myself. Here was a character who shared my radical views and my sense of humour. I skimmed ahead until a passage on Cyprus caught my eye, for negotiations between the Turks and the Greeks over Cyprus had been in the news only days before:

*...we anchored in a pretty little bay off the town of Limassol. Cyprus belongs to England, but the inhabitants are mostly Greeks and Turks. There are asbestos mines here and many people are employed at them, in fact these mines are the principal industry. There is a small trade done in Cyprus wines but I think it is purely local. We were fortunate in meeting a gentleman who had been to England and graduated from Oxford University. He had taken over his father's wine business but I am afraid he was a poor wine merchant as he contemplated selling off the remains of his stock and going to England to try and find a situation. He was a lover of the arts and dabbled in literature and was a member of the English Antiquarian society and posed as an expert on Greek*

5

*antiquities. We helped him to get rid of a small portion of his stock of wine and then had a look round his house and garden and then we went for a walk in the country around Limassol.*

*The town is very clean and the people are mannerly and well dressed. The police are fine looking men and to see them mounted on their sturdy ponies with a repeating rifle slung on their shoulders, they look very business-like indeed.*

I imagined my grandfather going around observing the local life in the Lancaster's various ports of call while his shipmates searched for the bars or the brothels. He seemed to have a novelist's eye for the people and their customs and evidently engaged with his imaginary reader. What reader did he have in mind, I wondered? His family obviously and perhaps his shipmates for I discovered recently that a chief stoker on HMS Lancaster had written out a complete copy of the diary for himself.

I was intrigued by his pungent criticisms of the Navy and its administrators:

*Most of my readers are aware that liquor of all kinds are denied to the lower deck (except the daily spirit ration of half a gill of rum) so that everyone from a Chief Petty Officer becomes a compulsory teetotaler between the times of being allowed ashore. The Navy is years behind the Army in this respect, and no matter in what part of the world one meets a soldier, one can bet his bottom dollar he is not far from a good copious supply of beer. There is absolutely no reason why a sailor should be denied the privilege of having beer, except that of precedent. Nelson's sailors had no beer allowed when they won the skirmish at Trafalgar. How dare sailors ask for or expect beer now? The Admiralty has been*

6

*approached on several occasions on this subject but, as usual, has listened to the crank in preference to the voice of common-sense. Drunkenness, Crime, Mutiny, Horrors!!!*

*Bakeries were strenuously opposed by those in authority as being impractical until we bought two ships from the Chilean Government called the Triumph & Swiftsure. These ships were fitted out with bakeries and even with them the experiment was not encouraged because, instead of sending bakers to work them, ship's cooks were sent, who, let them be what they may, are certainly not bakers. Handicapped as they were, the ship's cooks turned out tolerable bread and today no one would be so bold as to say that bakeries are in any way a failure and, if they cared to tell the truth, would tell you that the introduction of bakeries has been one of the greatest reforms in the Navy during the last quarter of a Century.*

I laughed out loud when I came to a passage in which he mocked naval customs by suggesting that a ship be towed behind each warship for the benefit of those cranks among naval officers who are obsessed with brass work and outer show. This sounds positively Monty Pythonesque:

*No one outside the navy can ever understand what a fetish paintwork & brightwork is in the Navy. Officers have placed the worship of this idol on a higher plane than the devotion of the heathen to his favourite joss. Admirals have bowed to it, and by its scarcity or otherwise so is a ship in their opinion efficient or morally decadent. A good way to deal with these paint & brightwork worshippers would be to have a special ship built for them carrying brass cannons. There would be nothing for use, everything being reserved for*

7

*show and she would be towed behind an ordinary ship in times of peace. Whenever an officer or man became tainted with paint or brightwork mania he would immediately be sent aboard and made to rub & scrub and feast and glut himself and after a fixed time of this treatment if no improvement was noted he could be sent to Yarmouth as an incurable. In the event of war, the tow rope could be severed and the ship and her crew with their paint & brightwork, turks-heads and brass cannon left to convince the enemy that they were to be reckoned with as "hot stuff".*

I was so absorbed in these pages that I had to be summoned several times to have lunch with my sisters. Little did I know as I poured out to them my excitement about his writing and his views that five years later I would not only follow his journey through his written words but that I would actually follow him to the places he visited a hundred years before.

After the meal my sisters and I pried open a drawer in mother's bureau which had been jammed shut for many years. Inside we discovered a treasure trove of photographs most of which we had never seen: early ones of our great grandparents, of my grandmother with my mother and her brothers as children and of my father and mother before their marriage. Then two photographs of James McKay: one a studio portrait of him dressed in formal naval uniform, the other of him in the garden at Errol holding his infant daughter (my mother) in the air with my grandmother looking on adoringly. His face is slim with finely defined features; his expression is serious, gazing intently at the camera. Just a hint of a smile in the family one; I detect a twinkle in his eyes which reminds me of my twin uncles. His service record notes that he was 6 feet in height, had dark brown hair and grey eyes with a fresh complexion.

My sisters, who were as excited as I was about this find, both live in London so we value the occasions when we can reminisce together about our family. Here was just such an opportunity. Mother had met our father at the University of Edinburgh where she was doing a postgraduate diploma in Social Studies and he was a junior lecturer in Classics. After a walk together through the old part of the city he suggested dropping in to a nearby restaurant for tea. She noted inwardly that it was one of Edinburgh's expensive places. After a substantial high tea she noticed him searching for his wallet and becoming increasingly concerned. She slipped him the money under the table, and made sure thereafter always to carry sufficient funds to cover expenses and to pay her bus fare home. She was a practical, canny Scot. She would occasionally tease my father for his English ways; he was born and raised in Liverpool in a middle-class family.

Dad was appointed to a permanent lectureship at Leeds University soon after my mother graduated in 1932. They married in 1936 and I was born a year later. Then came a life-changing event for all three of us: Dad was appointed Professor and Head of the Department of Classics at Rhodes University in South Africa. A notable achievement, for he was only twenty-nine. Fate intervened again. Before travelling to South Africa my parents were involved in a traffic accident on the way to a concert in London with another couple. Mother was the most seriously injured; she was thrown forward onto the back of the front seat and cracked her skull. She was concussed, and her forehead bore the indentation of that blow for life. The injury meant that she and I were unable to travel to South Africa with father so we spent the next year with relatives. According to mother, her mother doted on me. I was her first grandchild. Grandmother was heartbroken when mother and I eventually left for South Africa, for she believed that she would never see us again. She was right. I was eighteen months old when we joined Dad in Grahamstown and four when grandmother McKay died of coronary thrombosis at sixty-three. Mother was not able to travel to Scotland for her funeral because of the war which, the three of us agreed over the dining table, must have added to her grief.

The family grew to include my two younger sisters but we were isolated from our English and Scottish relatives by distance and then by the Second World War. Our only contact with them was through annual Christmas or birthday presents and the flimsy blue air letters. I heard very little about them except their names and occasional snippets about their doings read out from the letters. In later years after I had left home, my mother did talk to Kate, my younger sister, about our grandmother; she described her mother as stoic in the face of tragedy, never giving way to emotion; who would buy few clothes but always of good quality. Kate remembers mother holding her up as an example of survival without complaint. Kate said she was aware of our mother's hidden pain and distress when she spoke of her mother. We could not remember mother talking much about her father. His death at 33 had left the family struggling financially and, I would imagine, emotionally. In addition to my mother, who was four, there were twin boys born in the year he died. Grandmother went back to work as a seamstress, since her naval pension did not amount to much.

Those early years of poverty affected my mother deeply; she was thrifty and canny with money even when she and my father were comfortably off in South Africa. She would send me off on my bicycle as a primary schoolboy with used envelopes of cash in exact amounts to pay the household bills rather than waste money on cheques and postage. She made sure I collected all the receipts. I felt important and learned the importance of paying accounts promptly. Mother never talked about the grief that the young McKay family must have experienced. As a boy of ten I remember being shocked at her bursting into tears in front of her mother's grave stone in the village of Errol north of Dundee where she was brought up. This was the one and only time I saw my mother openly weep. I believe it was a bursting through of the grief which must have surrounded her at six and its resurgence over her mother's unexpected death.

My grandfather was born and raised in the tiny Highland village of Craigellachie, the third of thirteen children born to Peter and Helen McKay. His father worked as a forester on the estate of Sir Ronald Menzies and the family lived in a small cottage adjoining the local pub, the Fiddichside Inn. The garden stretched down to the River Fiddich. The Glenfiddich Distillery, built by William Grant and his sons in 1886, lies in the river valley at Dufftown four miles upstream. I visited Craigellachie in 2005 to get a feel for grandfather's home and found the Inn still flourishing but no adjoining cottage. The vacant space now serves as a parking lot for the InnThe present owner, Dot Brandie, told me that the cottage had fallen into ruin some years before. She is a youthful-looking woman of 92 with twinkling eyes who took over from her mother after the Second World War. She and her husband manage the bar; in fact he was serving behind the counter wnen I came in. She had to be summoned from "upstairs" to meet me. He had been told about the McKay family next-door but they had left before he married Dot. On the other hand, she remembered the McKays well, although James had died before her parents took over the inn in 1919. Her face lit up when I showed her a photograph of the McKays; my great-grandmother, Helen, had been like a mother to her. In fact Dot called her "Mum" and described her as "a jewel: the kindest person you could wish to know. She and my mother were great friends; if one of us children fell down and grazed a knee she would pick us up on her lap, bandage us and give us a sweetie." There was always music in the house next door, Dot said, especially on family occasions when Nellie, James' younger sister would play the piano "beautifully" and all would join in singing or playing an instrument. Jim's younger brothers were "warriors" who once set fire to the shed. Helen had the gift of second sight and had had a vision of James' body being tumbled around in the water the evening before his disappearance was reported in 1914.

After I ordered a second pint of Tartan ale, Dot told me about her days serving in the WRAF (Womens Royal Air Force) during World War 2. She ran upstairs to find a photograph of herself in uniform and propped it up on the bar so that I could photograph her with it. She became teary eyed as she talked about some of her colleagues who had not survived the war. However she still sees one who she had been talking to on the phone when I arrived that morning.

James McKay had no love of the sea or for ships; he joined the Royal Navy merely out of expediency:

*Much has been written about the glories and the mysteries of the sea. Poets and novelists have woven yards of romance around it but I am not writing this from any romantic point of view but from the standpoint of one, who driven by economic pressure was forced to adopt it as a means of livelihood. A Captain whom I had served under in a previous ship once told the assembled ship's company that if we were not in the Navy we would very likely be in the workhouse or prison. Apart from the insult contained in the assertion there was more truth in it than was meant to be conveyed. For what guarantee has a man possessing only his own labour that he will be able to sell it to an employer? We have in England close on one million unemployed which only serves to show how much we as a nation have to learn in the matter of organizing industry. In the ranks of the unemployed you will find the aristocrats of labour: tradesmen of all sorts who could be employed in doing useful work and producing wealth instead of being a burden on the lucky number who are favoured with employment. With a train of thoughts like these in my mind my reader must excuse me if I fail to rhapsodize about the blue and green of the ocean or its stately waves or mill-pond appearance.*

After he had served his apprenticeship and qualified as an engine fitter he found it difficult to get a job. Unemployment in Scotland was high, particularly amongst skilled engineers and shipyard workers. The Scottish historian T.M. Devine in *The Scottish Nation* reports that "shipbuilding and the other capital goods industries were subject to intense and savage fluctuation in 1884-1887, 1894, 1903-1905 and 1908." On Clydeside in 1908, 20% of the engineers and

13

almost 25% of the shipyard workers were out of work. Poverty and the associated diseases of tuberculosis, typhoid and respiratory failure were rife. Infant mortality rose from 118 per 1000 live births in the late 1860's to 130 in the late 1890's." The severity of this rate is evident when we compare the world rates for 2009; only four countries have higher rates- - Liberia, Afghanistan, Sierra Leone and Angola. My grandfather signed on for a 12 year stint in the Navy in 1903. He was 21 years old. The occupation listed on his service record is engine fitter and his first job was Acting Engine Room Artificer (ERA). His job entailed engine maintenance and organizing a group of stokers to feed the boilers with coal. He served in this capacity in several other vessels.

At the outbreak of the First World War in August 1914, James McKay was recalled from his shore job as an instructor to serve as an Artificer Engineer on HMS Pathfinder, a light cruiser. While patrolling off the coast of Scotland on September 5th, 1914 the Pathfinder was torpedoed by a German submarine with a direct hit on the engine room and the magazine. The force of the combined explosion tore the ship in two and she sank in about five minutes, taking my grandfather and about 260 shipmates with her. This was the first torpedo in history to sink a warship, in the second month of the war.

The small stone church in Craigellachie has a monument inscribed with the names of my grandfather and the 14 other men from the village and district who "fell" in the Great War. His name is also listed on the Roll of Honour together with nearly 150,000 Scots who died in that conflict at the Scottish National War Memorial in Edinburgh Castle. Apart from some possesions of his I now have - his cocked hat in a metal case, the two photographs, a brass plaque with his name from his sea chest and a framed scroll in the name of George V - my sole connection to my grandfather is through his diary. The injunction on the scroll: "Let those who come after see to it that his name not be forgotten" filled me with a desire to preserve his memory for future family and others through his own words rather than through a diary gathering dust in a museum library.

*I returned to my ship on the morning of the 30<sup>th</sup> and met a good many who were to be my future mess mates. We had orders to have our chests and bags in readiness and to muster at one o'clock for inspection by the Commodore. This spasm lasted an hour and then we had tea in barracks and four o'clock saw our belongings on the move and, a few minutes later, turning our backs to the stone frigate, we marched through the Dockyard and climbed over the gangway to the ship which was to be our home for the next two years. We went below and inspected our mess and bathroom, as the size and comfort of these mean so much to life aboard and, as they came up to our expectations, we returned on deck and saw our chests and bags unloaded from the cart and gave a hand to pilot them through various awkward passages to their berth in the mess-flat.*

*We now looked round for some food and, thanks more to our predecessors than to those in authority, found some in the shelves. When a ship is commissioned there are two old Navy customs which must be religiously observed; the first is that no food shall be served out the day of commissioning and the second that no leave shall be granted. We were lucky as*

15

*far as food was concerned and, after satisfying our material wants, we had a look round and grabbed a locker in the mess and bath, unpacked our chests and sought a billet to sling our hammocks, the latter being our dearest friends throughout a commission.*

*We turned in and slept the sleep of the just, tumbling out at 6:15 next morning to a wash and a fairly good breakfast. We then mustered outside the engineer's office to be detailed for our various duties but, owing to the senior engineer being absent, we spent the day exploring the engine rooms and stokeholds. A mess meeting was held in the afternoon to decide on rules to govern our conduct in the mess. The senior chief gave us some good fatherly advice and I thought that, if we acted up to the spirit of his remarks, we should get on fairly well together as a body of men. Leave being granted, the natives went ashore and I, being detained aboard for duty, spent the evening in reading and writing a few letters. A buzz that the Commander in Chief was coming aboard to inspect the ship & crew went round early in the evening and later on was verified by a message to the mess to muster in our best clothes on the following morning to receive His Eminence the Admiral.*

*We fell in for inspection by our own officers the next morning at nine o'clock and, by the time the various divisions had been formed up and instructed in the art of removing their caps in a way guaranteed to please the most fastidious of admirals, a bugle call announced the arrival of Admiral Drury and staff.*

16

Drury was a Canadian from New Brunswick who joined the Royal Navy and had a distinguished career there, becoming its second in command in 1903. At the time Grandfather began his voyage in 1910 he was a full Admiral in charge of the Chatham base and its surrounds.

*As the Admiral stepped over the after gangway he returned the salute of the Captain and officers, who were drawn up on the quarter deck awaiting him. The band played two measures of a salute and, these ceremonies ended, the inspection began. As the old sailor walked along between the lines of the divisions, his glance would wander from right to left as if seeking for some detail of dress that didn't correspond to Clause II of the clothing regulations. Occasionally he would stop and survey some individual from top to bottom and those who craned their necks to see how their shipmate behaved under such an ordeal were disappointed if they expected to witness a scene, for the Admiral passed right round the whole division without even a grunt or any sign of approval or displeasure. After leaving the upper deck he made a quick tour of the mess-decks and flats and shortly after took his departure.*

*We got into a working rig and, as the forenoon was well advanced, we made a party in the after stokehold to discuss our last ships and await the arrival of tot-time. After dinner, the senior engineer having arrived, we went round the ship in company with him and another engineer lieutenant to glean all necessary information for lighting up and getting under way. In the meantime permission had been requested to raise steam and try main and auxiliary machinery the following day, so that everyone in the engineer's department would have a chance to see how things behaved under steam before venturing on the trip to Gibraltar.*

*Leave was granted but I was one of four volunteers to stay aboard for duty and, as permission had been granted to try propelling machinery, we received orders to be below at 5 a.m. to light up and open out for steaming. After a struggle we managed to get everything in readiness for moving main engines and all having mustered in the Engine Room, each Engineer Officer & Engine Room Artificer had a trial as moving engineer to get his hand in so as to enable him to carry out the real orders with confidence and dispatch, which would come from the bridge on the morrow. These instructions filled up the forenoon and after dinner a look round the distilling plant completed the day's programme.*

*No leave was granted so after tea the next day, we gathered on the upper deck to watch the stir and bustle of getting a big ship ready for sea. We had moved in the afternoon into the north lock and only one caisson now barred our way to the River Medway. Articles of every description were arriving aboard. You would see one party humping great packing cases belonging to the officers; another party slinging a case in which reposed a motor car going to some Admiral in Malta; still another shouldering bales of straw which was to serve as litter for twelve dogs taking passage to Gibraltar. Various rumors were afloat concerning the ultimate destination of those dogs. One yarn was to the effect that they belonged to Scott's Antarctic Expedition and that we would trans-ship them at Gibraltar to a boat going to New Zealand; another was to the effect that they were hunting dogs going for the pleasure of the elite at Gibraltar.*

18

*Numerous officers came aboard to take passage to the station for which we were bound but none of them called for any special comment except that three parsons who were among the number seemed to me to be far too many to have aboard a man-o-war, especially as I am rather superstitious and still believe in Jonahs. The eve of our departure slipped away quickly and, as we had previously been detailed in watches for steaming, had counted up to see which would be the lucky watch to have Sunday forenoon below. I don't know if the parsons had anything to do with it but I found my watch would have to clean and attend divisions and divine service. This has developed into such a disagreeable way of spending Sunday forenoon that ninety nine out of every hundred in the engineer's department would rather go and work below.*

*The eventful morning of the 3<sup>rd</sup> arrived and promptly at 7:45 am we shoved our nose through the opening left by the removal of the caisson into the River Medway. The commission had really commenced and to celebrate the fact we were treated to a few selections from our band, the members of which were elated at the prospect as they were mostly natives of Malta and were really going home. We slipped down the river on whose bosom hundreds had passed at various times bearing their human cargoes to all the waters of the earth, past great battleships lying at anchor, whose crews cheered us as we crawled along, but many of us had little heart to return the compliment as only a few hours previous we had said goodbye to those who were very near and dear to us.*

*We dropped anchor near the Nase to take in ammunition & swing to adjust compasses. These duties were soon finished and at 10.30 we hauled up the mudhook and a* *few minutes later were en-route for Gibraltar. Just after noon we sighted and passed the "Terra Nova" on her voyage of discovery to the Antarctic regions. We exchanged signals and, as we were steaming at fourteen knots, soon left the sturdy little craft far astern. There is nothing particularly interesting in a voyage down channel as men of war keep well out from the land and the only objects noted are some well defined landmarks. Things went pretty smoothly in the engine room but, as we had shipped a good many $2^{nd}$ class stokers, without any previous experience of watch keeping or moving machinery, there were one or two slight accidents.*

*The morning of Sunday the $5^{th}$ found us well in the Bay of Biscay and the sea, which had been running pretty heavy during the previous day, had now become rough and the fishes had a good breakfast given gratis by the numerous sufferers from seasickness. Late on Sunday afternoon we picked up land on our port hand which I, not being a navigator, presumed to be the Coast of Spain. We had run closer to the beaten track of merchant ships, for we were sighting them frequently and I saw as many as six at one time. By ten o'clock in the evening the sea had gone down and the motion of the ship was almost imperceptible, just enough to lull one to sleep.*

*Nothing eventful happened on Monday except that about seven in the evening we were off Cape St. Vincent and we knew there were only 180 miles between us and Gibraltar. We eased down on Tuesday morning so as to bring us to anchor about nine o'clock at the end of the first stage of our journey. We sighted the rock, early in the morning standing out grim and bold; the gate of the Mediterranean, and exactly at nine o'clock the cable rattled through the hawse pipe and we swung gently round with the tide close to the entrance of the harbour of our nearest possession.*

*Gibraltar, like all Eastern places, looks splendid from a distance. The houses are brilliantly white and are covered with red tiles which glitter in the warm rays of the sun. Here and there glimpses of trees could be caught, while far away above the roofs of the houses, the rock threw its bare forehead away among the fleecy clouds hanging overhead.*

A hundred years ago it took HMS Lancaster four days to reach Gibraltar from England. Today the same journey takes less than three hours by air and the modern traveler thinks nothing of making trips of eight hours to cross the Atlantic from London to New York or even twenty two hours to fly half way round the world to Sydney in Australia. I imagine that such a world view would have been completely incomprehensible to James McKay or to almost anyone of his generation. I am intrigued with the differences in people's perceptions that must have resulted from this cognitive shrinking. Our inner maps and our sense of time and space must surely have undergone a radical shift over the past hundred years.

## CHAPTER 2: GIBRALTAR

I had planned to fly from Scotland to Portugal and Spain in search of Grandfather's ports of call but a family emergency dictated that I return to Canada. After dealing with the crisis I flew to Spain where I spent the first week of November 2005 at a training camp for scullers on the beautiful Guadalquivir River that runs through the centre of Seville. The last outing through the old city was on the Saturday morning. I took sad leave of the group I had grown close to over the week and, at 11, I was packed and ready to pick up my rental car for a weekend in Gibraltar, retracing the voyage of my grandfather. He describes a number of visits to that great naval base on the eve of the First World War. Not only was Gibraltar of strategic importance to the Royal Navy but it also provided them with a coaling depot and a capacious dry dock for repairs.

My first stop after leaving Seville was in Jerez in the south west - about a third of the way to Gibraltar - where my plan was to have lunch and visit the Gonzalez Byass plant which produces Tio Pepe, my favourite sherry. Alas, it was not to be. After a great meal of tapas and sherry on an outdoor terrace I proceeded to grapple with signs and road works in the centre of Jerez. Frustration! Three times I found myself back at the same barrier where the road simply ended in a large hole. I abandoned Tio Pepe. Inadvertently, I also abandoned the direct route to Gibraltar and found myself on the minor road which meanders along the Atlantic coast. That was the way I had intended to return to Seville so I resigned myself to the reversal. It was not without its rewards. As the road climbed through the coastal mountains I was stunned to see acres of wind turbines, their arms turning steadily in the breezy corridors between the hills; I thought immediately of Don Quixote. What would he have made of this army of giants? Would he have drawn his sword, spurred his steed and charged at them with his lance or would he have turned tail and run for it? I suspect he would have gone on the attack just as Cervantes described, for his spirit seems to live on in Spain where the people have thrown off the yoke of Franco's Fascism and repeatedly called their recent governments to account with strikes and protests.

After the road had followed the edge of the waves for some way, there were more swooping hills until suddenly there **IT** was – the Rock dominant in the distance. It was a truly awesome sight: A Pillar of Hercules indeed. I arrived at my hotel in La Linea just a kilometer from the customs post separating the British territory from Spain and, what luck! the Rock was visible from my room. It attracted me like a magnet so, without so much as unpacking, I registered, dumped my backpack in my room and walked along the seafront towards Gibraltar.

Customs and immigration were formalities: bored Spanish and Gibraltarian officials barely glanced at my passport. Just beyond the border there was the familiar sight of a red double-decker bus: *Hop on, hop off to the City Centre for a pound.* Sterling and Union Jacks – how British it all is, I thought. Climbing the steps from the city terminus the first thing I saw was a memorial to those who died in the First World War. I had tears in my eyes and a sob in my throat as I thought of his short life ending in that war. It was 6 in the evening. Here is his account of his first evening in Gibraltar in 1910:

*We got ashore about seven in the evening and made our way to the Naval Canteen where the Concert Party of H.M.S. London was giving an entertainment in aid of the Fresh Air Fund. As a rule there is not much attraction for me at any Naval institution as the irksome routine of the service is still in evidence and if one desires a pint of beer it has to be lowered down under the supervision of a patrol or a member of the Scotland Yard brigade. The one at Gib is the exception though, for the beer was nicely served and only tuppence a pint.*

*Afterwards we rambled about the streets for an hour or two, and we enjoyed the stroll very much. The narrow streets of Gibraltar are picturesque and the human elements of those streets are fascinating - one meets there so many foreign types. There are Spanish girls the exact counterparts of Carmen, with flashing black eyes and creamy skins, dressed in Spanish costumes and black mantillas, each with a red rose in her hair. There are Moors; black moors, in turbans and fezzes, with flowing cloaks, and curly daggers and the baggiest of breeches. There are bearded Jews in long white gabardines; muleteers and water-carriers and foreign and British sailors out of all the seas. Swarthy, piratical looking Maltese and Italians with rings in their ears rub shoulders with panama-hatted, white drill-clothed English and American visitors from the calling ships. I saw gypsies on shaggy ponies, grooms on officers' chargers and Spanish wagons built on lines as*

24

*gracious as those of Drakes' ships of war which pass like figures in a play. We retraced our steps in the direction of the harbour and, looking across the smooth stretch of water, we could see the twinkling lights of Algeciras. Glancing further round to the right we saw Lenia, a town famous in the eyes of Navy people as being the nearest town to Gibraltar where a real Spanish bull fight can be witnessed.*

I stood in John Mackintosh Square (formerly the Piazza) with the staid City Hall at one end and the British Colonial style Parliament building at the other admiring its sense of space. I then walked along Main Street seeing it all through his eyes. The pubs, churches and public buildings he would have recognized but not the huge plate glass window displays of Marks & Spencer's and British Home Stores. I wandered through the maze of cobbled lanes with polished pavements winding uphill from Main Street which would have been more familiar to him.

I found a quiet courtyard at the end of one lane. I realized that I was hungry; it was 7.30 and almost dark. The only sounds were of children chasing each other through the square. At one end of the square there was a Moroccan restaurant. The proprietor opened the door as I arrived. I chose a table under the leafy boughs of a huge tree and the proprietor himself served me a traditional Moroccan dish of couscous and lamb baked in a pie plate covered with a domed lid with a side salad and a glass of wine. The night was like crystal with a deep indigo sky. Lights illuminated the square. The feet of passers by clicked or shushed on the polished stone tiles; I saw dark faces in burqas, a grey-bearded Jew with his prayer shawl under his arm and then a younger man also with a shawl, probably both on their way to the synagogue. Two red-shirted "Team Gibraltar" boys with water guns chasing and hiding from each other whooped it up. They turned out to be part of the restaurant owner's family. One or two tourists with their inevitable baseball caps strolled by. The night was warm and still. Darkness had descended over the city suddenly as it does in sub-tropical climates. I wandered back to the bus stop through well-lit, deserted streets.

Sunday was a perfect day for climbing the Rock on foot as Grandfather had done all those years ago. Under a cloudless, azure-blue sky I could see the contrast between present day Gibraltar and the skyline with red-roofed white houses and trees grandfather described in 1910. It has altered dramatically. High rise apartment blocks, condominiums and hotels swarm up the lower slopes. Most residents live in these tower blocks as there are few detached houses for the thirty thousand people crammed into the space squeezed between the Rock and the water. As a result, the city has one of the densest populations in the world.

The territory of Gibraltar covers the 6.8 square kilometer southern tip of Spain. It has been occupied by many invaders, most recently by the British, who have ruled it since 1713. Spain has besieged it, isolated it and quarrelled over it at the United Nations and the European Union in order to regain sovereignty over it. Strategically it has been important over the ages (and continues to be) since it stands at the narrow Western entrance to the Mediterranean basin. Ever since establishing a naval base on Gibraltar over three hundred years ago, the Royal Navy has been a major contributor to the economy; in 1984 the Royal Navy contributed sixty per cent of Gibraltar's national income. Twenty years later that percentage had fallen to seven. Tourism, commerce and shipping are now the major economic resources.

Gibraltarians are a population of diverse origins: 27% have British ancestry; 26% Spanish and 19% Italian. The official language is English but one hears Spanish, Arabic, Hindi and Shindhi on the streets. There is also an indigenous language known as *Llanito.* which mingles Andalucian, English and Maltese. I noticed laundry and Union Jacks hanging all over the city. Construction is booming, with huge cranes constantly at work. Indeed Gibraltar struck me as a city in which the concrete never sets. Since it was Sunday the streets and lanes were quiet; shops all shut except for the odd newsagent/novelty kiosk. I stopped at one to get directions for climbing the Rock. The owner turned out to be a third generation Gibraltarian with an Indian background who told me with pride about his home.

"Was Gibraltar likely to revert to Spain?" I asked.

"Not if we have anything to do with it – even if the British wanted to hand it over."

I heard this sense of being a Gibraltarian repeated by others I talked to; later I discovered that the entire civilian population was evacuated to  England, Morocco and other countries during the Second World War and that their exile had given birth to this sense of national pride. Something grandfather would not have encountered.

The hike up the Rock was a long slog compensated by wonderful views of the harbour growing more diminutive by degrees. Rounding one bend I saw the clear view across the straits to Morocco 15 kilometres away. There stood the second Pillar of Hercules. Since it was only 10 in the morning there were few cars and no other pedestrians. The roadway was tarred and eventually narrowed from a two lane road to a one-way system. One intriguing feature was a series of metal rings set at intervals into the rock at the side of the road. I later found out that these had been used in the 1700's by the British to drag heavy cannons to the batteries at the summit. Mules and men had hauled them up in stages. From reading my grandfather's account more carefully I realized that I had chosen a southern route whereas he describes a zigzag dirt path skirting the Moorish castle on the north end of the rock. No matter, I would go up again later since I wanted to explore the 8th Century walls and the castle. I climbed beyond the huge caves of St. Michael where the British forces had constructed an indoor city during WW2 complete with power station, hospital and accommodation for an entire army and its ancillaries. Churchill had ordered it built to resist the potential Nazi or Spanish invasion which would have meant losing the Allies' strategic key to the Mediterranean. About a hundred meters from the summit I found the roadway blocked and the area fenced off. I suppose the signal station at the top is still of strategic significance. So I was not able to see over the sheer cliff to the Mediterranean side as grandfather was able to do. I did see the British Naval base in the harbour and the coaling wharf he mentions. I also made acquaintance with the famous Rock Apes. Tawny in colour they only seemed interested in humans for their food value and, since I had been warned not to conceal any snacks about my person, I was more interested in them than they in me. I tried several alternative paths down the mountain but eventually had to retrace my morning route. I stopped for lunch at the outskirts of the city but did not bury my face in a beer as grandfather later describes; I drank a cool glass of white wine. I had been en route for almost four hours.

Refreshed, I set out for the climb up to the Moorish castle on the north side of the town. I walked into several dead end streets and had to retrace my steps. No signposts. But about half way up, the route started to zigzag as grandfather had described and I found a rough path leading off the tarred roadway. It was half hidden in the undergrowth. Something seemed to compel me to follow it; I picked my way carefully along the edge of the cliff. Unlike the roadway it was utterly deserted and I had great views down to the castle and the ancient defensive walls. The path led to the ruins of a gun emplacement where I paused and sat down to catch my breath. I imagined my grandfather climbing the Rock and resting here on this very parapet. What would it be like to meet him? What would we say to each other? What would he be like? I shut my eyes and relaxed my body with deep breathing. I could picture him sitting along the wall from me in his dark blue uniform. It feels eerie; a shiver goes up my spine

"No need to be afraid," he would say in a soft Highland burr, "I was permitted to meet you here."

As I look into his clear blue eyes he seems familiar: his voice and his accent, remind me of Uncle Jim, my mother's younger brother. As if catching my thought:

"Aye, I am also Jim, Jim or James McKay, his father."

"Grandfather!" I blurt out, "But how is this possible?"

"It was you who opened the door, James, with your focus on me and the intense feelings you have had since you read my

29

journal and started to follow my journey. When you, a grandson I never knew, set out to discover me I received a form of dispensation to return to you in spirit. This is given to people who have strong feelings one for another, d'you see? So you have conjured me up in a place I enjoyed in the form I was when I was a visitor here all those years ago."

I look at him in stunned silence while he gazes back at me steadily, waiting for my incredulity to settle. As I had so often sat and stared at his photograph, it was easy to imagine what he looks like. I see a man of medium height with a fair complexion etched with worry lines. He looks older than his 29 years. His peaked cap with its gold embroidered anchor and crown is carefully whitened. He is clean shaven with even features and the soft lines around his eyes display his sense of humour. His jacket is formal – double-breasted with six shiny buttons. Under it he wears a crisp white shirt with a dark blue cravat showing at the collar. His left thumb is tucked into a pocket; below the jacket he has matching serge trousers and well-shined ankle boots.

As if reading my thoughts once more: "Too cold a wind for my tropical uniform today; this is the only warm outfit I have. And, aye, I am able to read your mind - one of the perks of the afterlife. But dearie me! How Gibraltar has changed."

He gets up from the low wall and gazes down to the north where the road to Spain runs next to a football pitch.

"In my day that was acres of waste ground. It was known as the neutral zone – a kind of no-man's land separating British territory from Spanish. Now it is filled with those strange tall buildings – d'ye call them skyscrapers?"

"Not really, they are just called high rises now, grandfather. Skyscrapers would be more like 60 storeys; these are mainly about 6 to 10 storeys. Most of them are hotels and flats."

He notices the line up of cars at the airstrip: "What are all those cars and buses waiting for? Why are there gates at that cross road?"

"That is not a cross road where those cars are held up; that's an airstrip. See, there is a plane taking off."

We watch in silence as a miniature-looking British Airways plane flies off on its trip to London.

He looks stunned: "I do remember the first manned flight in 1903 by the Wright brothers in America. But this...... When was that airstrip built?"

"During the Second World War so the Allies could transport troops here in a hurry and fly squadrons of fighter planes against the Germans. Its major function these days is bringing hordes of tourists here coming for the sunshine and the good life. Many British people retire here to escape taxes and the high cost of living at home."

"So that's a major industry for the inhabitants now? Instead of serving ships and sailors they serve the wealthy classes?"

"That's right – and workers from Spain cross the border every day to supplement local labour," I reply. "The resorts and hotels are run by international cartels and are not owned by the locals."

"So the profits leave the country for the benefit of capitalists?" he asks.

"That's right. The class system is just as strong as it was in your day but now multinational companies own the wealth; some have more clout than individual countries."

"Fascinating – and frightening," he says.

"Grandfather, do you see those high rise buildings on the far side of the airstrip?"

"Aye – you mean where no-man's land used to be?"

"Yes that is La Linea where the hotel that I am staying in is. You saw it on your first night here." He looked puzzled. "Do you remember? You wrote that it was known to sailors as the nearest place where they could see a bullfight and you called it Lenia."

"Och aye; I remember now but how different the buildings look from the shabby wee houses that were there then. I suppose this is what they call progress?"

"Something like that. And another change from your day is the pride people have in calling themselves Gibraltarians. You spoke of all the various nationalities you encountered here - Moors, Spaniards, Jews, Maltese and Italians - as though there were no people of the Rock."

"That's true; they all seemed to be temporary, almost as though they were waiting for Gibraltar to be handed back to Spain."

"Well not any longer; most of those I met are fiercely independent and resist any notion that they will become Spanish. They have their own government and are independent from Britain except for foreign affairs and defense."

I tell him of my encounters with locals and what I had learned about their wartime evacuation and its part in fostering the new sentiment of pride.

"James, but now it is time for me to leave you as I am only allowed a limited time. However, I will be able to join you again on your travels. Where do you expect to go next?"

"Probably Malta and Menorca," I reply. "Goodbye, grandfather."

He seems to fade away gradually rather than disappear suddenly.

Going down was harder on my legs than the climb up had been. In fact my calf muscles were still stiff days later! I rested in the beautiful surroundings of the Botanical Gardens which were known as the Alameda in grandfather's day. Sitting under a pine tree in the gathering dusk, I read his account of a night in Gibraltar and his climb up the Rock the following day.

*On the evening of Tuesday the 2ⁿᵈ of August we steamed through the breakwater at Gib and tied up at the old billet, alongside the coaling wharf. The starboard watch went on leave at noon the following day and as a months' money* had just been paid the boys were determined that they would fully enjoy themselves; and judging by the text our Scotch minister chose while preaching to the troops on the following Sunday, they had done themselves fairly well. The text or rather the words on which he hung his discourse were, "Be sure your sin will find you out". He assured us that no specific reference was conveyed in those few words to the doings of the previous week while the boys were ashore and though I believed him I am sorry to think that thousands wouldn't.

I went on my leave on the Friday afternoon along with two companions and, after a stroll through the Alameda Gardens, had a walk to Europa Point and inspected some of the batteries and fortifications. We stayed that night at the house of a villainous looking Spaniard, who made us fairly comfortable, and in the morning, though we fully expected to have our throats cut, he let us go on payment of 2 shillings each. We had a whole day in front of us and after breakfast started off to climb to the top of the Rock. As the ascent can be made from different starting places we decided to commence our journey from the <u>Ramps.</u> (How I wish I could tell you about this wonderful place. Suffice for me to say that Ramps is a contraction for ramparts and everyone knows that in such a place you want an efficient weapon and a plentiful supply of ammunition.) Like the traveller in "Excelsior" as soon as we entered the ramps we had numerous offers from the charming residents to come and stay for a short time but as the day was hot and the path steep, we graciously waived their offers, promising to come some other time, and digging our toes into the hard soil we set a course for the Moorish Castle.

*As we slowly zig-zagged up the face of the famous rock we had to stop frequently and admire the magnificent scenery that lay around us. An hours' hard climbing took us to the signal station where, in the absence of something stronger, we refreshed ourselves with a copious draught of rain water and feasted our eyes on the glorious panorama spread out beneath and all around us. We were right on the ridge, and on the Mediterranean side, the rock dipped sheer down some hundreds of feet and then sloped gently away to meet the rippling waters of the Mediterranean. Nestling close to the foot of the rock and divided from the sea by a little belt of silver sand lay the small hamlet of Catalan. To the north, cut off from the rock by a narrow strip of soil, known as the neutral ground lay the historic land of Spain.*

*Many eyes, in different ages, have gazed wistfully across the line that divided them from the Rock, and in their hearts have cursed the race who wrenched it from them, and have wept to think that the once proud Spanish race, which, in earlier days had been looked upon as the most powerful in Europe, had degenerated to a race ruled by a weak monarch and a queen who bartered her principles for position and oppressed by a church which yearly threatened to break their backs. There are signs of an awakening, even in this decadent race. As shown by recent risings in Barcelona and other parts of Spain against the infamous war lately engineered by a few Spanish capitalists and mine owners against the Moors who, poor devils, naturally resented the stealing of their land by those grasping mercenaries. Away to the south lay the northern border of the great, dark, mysterious continent of Africa. The coast line is bold and rugged and in the fastness of the dark range of hills in the background are the homes of the brigand and his faithful troops. This quaint yet wonderful people are ruled by a Sultan, who has for his special benefit a harem of lovely girls; and we English with our mock modesty and false Christianity turn up our eyes to heaven and deplore such depravity; as witness the recent outcry against the Agapomone at Spaxton, and in our hearts are envious.* (Agapomone was a commune)

*Bringing our view nearer, the dockyard lay beneath us like a child's model, decked out with miniature ships. The Lancaster looked like a toy boat with three cigarettes as funnels, but a glance at her brought back visions of dirty coals and blistering heat and sweat and curses and, though no word was spoken, a cold shiver passed through us, as when a master cracks his whip over his slave or a murderers' hand closes round his victim's throat. We seemed to have no heart left for sight seeing after even so hurried a glance at the galley and seizing the visitors book, with trembling hand we inscribed our names and half running, half falling we arrived at the bottom safe and sound, though out of breath, and in a few minutes had our noses and half our heads buried in a mug of beer in an endeavour to shut out the horrible vision conjured up at the sight of the ship with the squashed tomato badge.*

*We sat and rested in this cafe for about an hour and watched the numerous visitors come and go and were compelled to admire the way in which the foreigners refreshed themselves. They do not indulge in beer or spirits to any great extent but sip peculiar colored drinks from grotesque looking bottles; the more temperate taking a glass of coffee and milk. The latter as made in Gib, I can thoroughly recommend as the Spaniards are connoisseurs of coffee and artists in serving it. The average Britisher who stows away about a gallon of beer*

36

*is a gross animal compared with his southern or continental brother. It would be interesting to watch the look on a publican's face in England if one asked for a glass of coffee or half a pint of tea. Temperance at home is not encouraged as you will find out for yourself if you care to ask for lemonade and be prepared to pay about seven times its value. We passed the remainder of the afternoon looking round the curio shops but being at the wrong end of the commission could not afford to buy any of the beautiful oriental goods (who said Brummagem?) displayed by the olive skinned Jews of the east.*

Sitting in the gardens with wonderful tropical perfumes in the air I thought about the passage above in which grandfather described looking down on HMS Lancaster and being reminded of the horrors of living on board and working in the overheated engine room. What a contrast to my life in the Mediterranean – luxurious hotels, comfortable air travel and good food. His life was so constricted by naval regulations and authoritative rules where I was free to travel where and when I wanted and to drink the whisky and beer he would have so enjoyed. Feeling sad for him I left the Botanical Gardens and made for my hotel in La Linea on the red double-decker bus and shank's pony.

Outside the hotel I was hailed by a woman who asked if I spoke English.

"Thank goodness," she said. "I have just been mugged and I need your help. Two dark-skinned men knocked me to the ground, took my purse, my cell phone and my money. The police don't think I have a hope of getting anything back and I have no way of getting home to my flat which is about 15 kilomctrcs. away. Do you have a car?"

I pointed to it and said I had maps so we could find the way together.

"Oh that would be too difficult as it's so dark. The taxi fare is 16 euros; could you lend me that? I will come to your hotel with it tomorrow."

She suggested we have a coffee so I took her to the lounge in my hotel where the coffee was free. In the light she did look disheveled; she was about 35, dark haired, slim and attractive with slit eyes. We talked about where we lived; she said she lived in Aberdeen although her accent was from the South of England. She had come to Spain for her sister's wedding to a Spanish doctor and had a flat for another few days. However she did not see any point in staying after this incident. I told her I would be leaving the hotel the following day and gave her my address in Canada so that she could send the money there. I gave her 20 euros as I did not have smaller change and she departed to catch her taxi. As I returned to my room, my suspicions grew. What if all this was a con? Perhaps she had accomplices nearby who would steal my rented car. What a palaver that would be. I decided to park the car in the underground garage and started to get ready for bed with a sense of relief.

As I was pulling the covers over myself, the telephone disrupted my calm. The only person who knew my number was my wife, Anne, so I answered it. The desk: "Sandy is in the lobby asking for you."

I protested that I was in bed but the clerk had rung off. With a heavy heart I went down.

"Thank God," she said grabbing my arm. "You'll never guess what has happened now. We can't talk here. What did you say your room number was?"

"403."

I followed her into the elevator feeling like a lamb led to the slaughter.

She sat herself down on the bed. "I got all the way there only to find the spare key which the landlady had put under the flower pot was missing. So I had no way of getting in – fortunately I managed to get the taxi to bring me back without a charge - wasn't that lucky?"

Now I was feeling scared. "So what do you want from me?"

She said she was hungry so would I order something from room service while she had a shower.

"And then are you planning to stay the night?" I asked.

"Well, what else can I do?"

I said I did not know but that I was not comfortable with her spending the night in my room.

"You don't trust me then? You think I invented all this."

I told her I had known her for a short time and that building trust took longer for me: no, I did not trust her.

"I think I have done what I can to help you so have your shower, eat your sandwich and then you must leave."

She protested that I would have all my money back and that her father owned a business in the area and she would see him the following day. In answer to my offer of the phone to call him she said that all her numbers were in the cell phone which had been stolen with her purse. She went off to have her shower and reappeared with her jeans carelessly unzipped. She laid her head on my lap. I had absolutely no interest in her advances. I wanted her out of my room ASAP.

She repeated her plea to stay. "If you don't trust me here is my address and my father's." She insisted on writing them in my day book. I was adamant that she was not going to stay, thinking of how vulnerable that would make me with passport, money and possessions disappearing while I slept.

"Well those people around me after I was mugged said I could get a hostel bed for E10."

I eventually gave her the money and saw her to the hotel door. I slept fitfully, still worried that I had not heard the last of Sandy, the con girl. I was sure that I had seen the last of my euros, though. My grandfather had done rather better than me at resisting the invitations of the charming residents of the ramparts. I mused about whether he could become a kind of guide or guardian angel for me on my travels; after all he had promised to meet up with me again. As I drove back to Seville to catch my return flight I pondered on the form this next connection might take. A month later and there has been no contact from Sandy since that disturbing Sunday night.

# CHAPTER 3: MALTA

Ancient, mythical, revered, spiritual.... those were the first impressions I had of Malta. Approaching the island by sea from the west (as Grandfather did) the capital, Valetta, rises from the soft blue of the Mediterranean, fortress-like. Limestone walls and bastions over one hundred meters high have withstood many invasions: from the Arabs and the Turks five centuries ago to the Nazi and Italian air forces in the Second World War. The city emerges from the stone battlements all domes and spires, on a promontory between twin harbours: the Grand Harbour and Marsamxett. The Grand Harbour was home to the Royal Navy for centuries and is now a busy commercial port and dockyard. Marsamxett is a forest of sailboat masts rising straight up from the clear water, revealing its recreational function. My friend Jay and I were staying in a small holiday hotel overlooking Marsamxett with a regular ferry service across the harbour with a steep climb up to the old city.

Everywhere scores of ancient Leyland diesel buses provide excellent chugging service across the island. The suburbs of Valetta merge into adjoining towns where half the population live and serve the scores of summer visitors. It's April, the "shoulder" of the season before the onslaught of tourists in May. The climate is friendly; a cool breeze softens the constant sun, and air-conditioning is not necessary. History and tradition predominate; but tourism is the new industry, and the cranes at the new construction sites dwarf the ancient buildings.

On Friday afternoon, a week to the day after leaving Chatham, we entered the Grand Harbour of Malta, passed Fort St. Elmo and picked up a buoy in Bighi Bay. If there be any truth in the saying the first impressions are best then I am sorry to say Malta as viewed from its harbour did not impress me very favourably. Looking from the ship we could see two fortresses, which are used as barracks for soldiers, an hospital perched on top of a rock, and that most indispensable place of detention, common to all civilised countries, namely a prison.

Lying in the harbour was a French man of war and just as we finished making fast to our buoy the Mediterranean fleet, which had been out for a few days, came steaming into harbour. As they came through the breakwater the French & English ships exchanged salutes and then they passed on to their respective buoys. Leave was granted till 7 o'clock on the following morning and was taken full advantage by those entitled to go ashore. The harbour presented a very animated appearance. No ships boats are allowed for liberty men and, as a consequence, there is a real competition amongst the Dyso-men for the privilege of landing the different ships' companies. Every ship has a number of them attached to her and they are supposed to be always in attendance on this particular ship. When the liberty men are ready to go, the ships dysos are drawn up round the gangway like cabs on the rank and as soon as one gets its load and pushes off another takes its place.

Numerous racing boats crews were out practising in the harbour and from among the throng one could pick out the army officers and dockyard officials enjoying the cool of the evening from the stern sheets of their private boats. I did not go ashore as it was late in the evening and I had promised *myself at least half a day on my first excursion so as to have ample time for a good look round. I was however, disappointed in my promised half holiday as we had to work on Saturday afternoon and I found I would be unable to go on Sunday on account of being duty watch so to satisfy my curiosity I went on shore on Saturday night along with a few messmates. The first individual we saw on the landing stage was a Roman Catholic priest and he was but the forerunner of many.*

*Valetta, where we landed, is built on rising ground and the sidewalks leading from the quay are merely steps of stone about 4 inches high and are extremely difficult to negotiate. The first object of interest we came to was a magnificent Roman Catholic Church. It seemed, viewed from the outside, to be of gigantic proportions and capable of holding all the people in Malta. Although it was seven o'clock in the evening it was lit up and, as the door stood open, we took it for granted that this was an invitation to enter. We passed through the great doors and gazing into the dimly lit interior we were struck with the vastness and splendour of our surroundings. The walls were covered with oil paintings and from numerous niches statuettes of saints seemed to keep guard over the treasures around them. Far away above our heads the domed roofs stretched resplendent in gilt and gold.*

*The church was crowded with devout worshippers and, fearing we might be intruding, we feasted our eyes on the splendour around us for a few brief moments and then passed quietly out into the street. We learned afterwards that this was the Cathedral of St. John, the principal church in Malta, and that at some remote period of history it had boasted of possessing gates of real gold but that they had been looted and carried away by the French when they captured the Island.*


With the help of the Maltese Tourist Office, I tracked down the owner of a dyso (dghaisa in Maltese), the small craft that grandfather described for rowing the crews of visiting ships ashore. I hired him to take me across to HMS Lancaster's mooring at Bighi Bay and row me back to the quay. Naturally oars are now ancillary to outboard motors so we putt-putted our way across the harbour. He was knowledgeable and was able to tell me how the various waterside buildings would have been used 100 years ago. He had restored his dyso to its former glory; it had been constructed in 1949 for the use of Princess (now Queen) Elizabeth on her visits to her fiancé Philip, who commanded HMS Magpie and quartered at the naval barracks near Bighi Bay on his leaves ashore. Intricate brass and wood carvings on the transom and gunwales included a symbolic red rose for its royal occupant. On each side of the bow were the ubiquitous alert eyes of Osiris, the Egyptian goddess, painted on the prow of every traditional Maltese craft to ward off evil. This custom dates back to Phoenician times, around 1500 BC. The current passenger, buoyed by the spirit of his grandfather, landed at the bottom of a winding set of stone steps leading up to the Co-Cathedral of St John in the centre of Valetta, which James McKay had visited on his first shore leave. He had found the steps awkward to negotiate as did I. Later I discovered the reason: they were designed for knights in full suits of armour. On the way up I saw a workman repairing one of the flagstones, carefully shaping the replacement to fit. Ornate doorways, some with Maltese crosses in the panels, were flanked by small terra cotta figures such as the Virgin Mary with an angel, St George slaying the dragon and on one home a sign, "God bless America" I passed two business men in suits and briefcases and a number of well-dressed women in high heels. There were few people on the stairways but lots of cats sunning themselves on front doorsteps.

The cathedral, which was completed by the Knights of Malta in 1578, is austere on the outside but ornate inside. Built of stone in the style of a fortress it has twin square towers with conical tops. These cone-shaped roofs are not symmetrical, for one cone is obscured by a set of bells hung from an arch which looked as though it had been added as an afterthought. A wide, curving set of steps led up the imposing double doors, looking out onto a beautifully proportioned square with restaurants, open air tables and shops. The Baroque interior took my breath away but, before I could take it all in, I was admonished by a priest for being too exposed for God. He provided me with an apron to cover my shorts and my bare legs. For shame!

The interior was not dark as it was in grandfather's time; electric light has made a difference. In fact, I was able to take photographs without using flash, which was forbidden anyway. Some of the gold leaf encrusted on the carved columns was worn off (or perhaps sold off) but rich paintings and murals were everywhere just as he described them. Dominating the high altar was a sculpture of John the Baptist baptizing Jesus and, in the Oratory, a painting over the altar by Caravaggio depicting St. John's beheading. The drama is stark: the executioner holds down the martyr's neck with his left hand, his right clutching an axe. An official in uniform behind him appears to be urging him to finish St. John off

45

while a female holds a wide salver to receive the victim's head. An old lady alongside the group clasps her head in horror at the sight. Caravaggio has signed the work in the blood oozing from the Baptist's neck. The painting, I discovered later, was the largest Caravaggio painted and the only one he ever signed. His other work is peaceful by contrast and depicts St Jerome writing, pen poised over his manuscript. However even he is watched by a human skull serving as a paperweight.

As to Jim's belief that half Malta could have fit into the church, I think the darkness must have misled him for, while it soared up to the dome above, I would not describe the interior as vast. Impressive nonetheless. The dome and the archways are completely covered with frescoes. The Knights certainly did go for baroque!

From the Cathedral, I walked round the corner to the Strada Reale which has been renamed Street of the Republic.

*Afterwards we took a stroll along the Strada Reale, which would correspond to our high street at home. Being Saturday night the scene was more animated than usual. Maltese ladies, with sparkling eyes and creamy skins, rustling in silks and laces with parasols of rainbow hue swung along in twos and threes chattering away in their native tongue. Priests of all shapes and sizes; big priests, lean looking priests worn out by penance and vow, priests with hats and priests with shaven pates passed and repassed until one wondered if the priests of the world had congregated here. English men and women were much in evidence but they seem to have developed a sort of snobbishness in this priest-ridden*

46

*community and keep themselves aloof from the natives and have their own clubs and institutions. Piratical looking Maltese men stood in groups at the street corners or walked about among the gay throng, chattering and gesticulating and seemingly enjoying themselves. They would occasionally stop at one of the numerous cafes where they sit and have their refreshment in full view of the passers-by.*

*This system of having refreshment practically in the open has much to recommend it as a man who takes a refresher has it at leisure and can watch the passing throng from a comfortable seat and at the same time is mindful that the eyes of the multitude are upon him and this very fact keeps him from imbibing too freely as no one likes to become a glutton in public. I think there is much room for improvement in this respect in England. There are no gardens even in summer where one can sit and listen to a decent band. Instead people have to congregate in dingy rooms amidst dismal surroundings and the only recreation provided is a dart or shove-ha'penny board with plenty of watery whisky and doctored beer to satisfy the craving of the inner man. Truly the English are a sporting race.*

Republic Street was crowded with locals and tourists rather than priests or pirate-like men although I did see one priest in a long black robe with a white girdle, a determined expression on his face, as though intent on rounding up a sinner.. Open air cafes and pubs abounded although the music pouring from them has changed significantly over the hundred years. In spite of the plate glass fronts and banking machines, I got a real sense of what he must have seen looking down the length of the street. The buildings, mostly limestone or sandstone, arc warm in tone, especially in the late afternoon sunlight when they become earthy orange in colour. Many still retain their original stone arches but their enormous doors have been replaced with shop front windows and smaller entrances. There are many British chain stores such as Marks & Spencers and Mothercare under the arches. Unusual features were the enclosed bump-out balconies from which occupants could view life on the street. On side streets I saw washing hung out to dry from the balcony windows; from one hung a family of small football jerseys. I was told that people are fanatical about the game.

The Maltese I met in different walks of life seemed, like the buildings, warm in character. A number of people I approached for directions insisted on taking me there, going out of their way to help a visitor. On one occasion, the bus driver was unable to change my note and motioned for me to get off. Overhearing this, two locals jumped to my rescue, producing the requisite fare, and I had to choose which offer to accept. When I recounted the episode to a taxi driver, he said: "We are all family on Malta." English is spoken everywhere since the Maltese lived under English rule for 250 years until they reached full independence in 1964. So being understood was no problem. I was told that English is taught as a second language in school and that many speak Italian and French as well. I found wait staff retain the dignity Grandfather attributes to the Maltese character. They are neither haughty nor servile as in some countries. There was a sense of fun and friendliness I encountered in my contacts.

*Our stay in Malta was not destined to be a long one as manoeuvres on an elaborate scale were to take place in English waters in which we were to play some small part. There was great excitement on board when the official news came that we were going to Falmouth to meet the other fleets taking part. A rumor, which spread like lightning, was to the effect that we should get five days leave before returning to the station. Even the fact, that we were to have an Admiral's inspection on the following Thursday, failed to damp the spirits of the more than usual depressed amongst us. This inspection was largely a farce and in this respect differed very little from the ordinary Admiral's inspection. Everything that might offend his eye was carefully hidden away; the brightwork got an extra polish and in fact he saw everything, not as they would be under ordinary working conditions but under conditions which might prevail on a yacht or any craft designed for pleasure and not for use.*

*However - it is an ill wind that blows nobody good and we benefited on this occasion to the extent of a half holiday. Along with several messmates I hied ashore and, wishing to have a look at the environs of Malta, we hired a gharry and drove to the famous gardens of San Anton.*

*On passing through the portals we were confronted with a view of a typical tropical garden and it surprised us to find a spot so green and beautiful in such a barren island where goats live on paper and holystones. The ordinary flowers and shrubs we took little notice of but confined our attention more to the strange tropical plants and shrubs everywhere in evidence. There were plenty of orange and lemon trees, the fruit on which was just forming. One of the party who had lived in Malta some time previous volunteered the information that the oranges grown at San Anton were the finest the world produced and that the Royal household in England was supplied from this source. Let that be as it may, I have my mind made up that, when the proper season comes round I shall try them for myself. We spent about an hour in looking round and then had a nice bottle of English beer in the garden of a public house near by. We then hailed our garry and arrived back in Valetta in time for our tea, which, by the way, we had at the house of a Maltese lady who had been recommended to us.*

San Anton Palace Gardens lie on the outskirts of Valetta at the end of a convenient bus route. I walked along its formal, gravel paths and looked up at the enormous trees all carefully labeled. Sounds of fountains and bird life filled the air. I spied groves of trees with lemons loading the leaves. The scent of orange blossom caught my attention; there were the trees he describes carefully fenced off from the public. Presumably the oranges would now go to the President rather than to English Royals because the 17th Century palace set in the gardens is now the residence of the President. Until independence in 1966 it was inhabited by the British Governor. The gardens and the palace are named for man who was Grand Master of Malta from 1623 to 1636, Antoine de Paule. He personally supervised the planting of flowers, shrubs and trees. Imagine my surprise over a cup of tea at a nearby café to hear a tremendous squeal from a cage containing a pair of wallabies with one small one en pouch! Truly the world has shrunk.

*We tied up to our respective buoys on Saturday forenoon inside the Grand Harbour after an absence of three months and were immediately seized upon by a horde of washer women, dyso-men and canteen pirates. There is an air of homeliness about Malta which appeals to the sojourners in the Mediterranean Fleet, and I went ashore on every available opportunity. I found out a good deal of the seamy side of life in Malta during our second visit, especially as regards prostitution and drunkenness. Any reader must not rush away with the idea that the Maltese are either immoral or addicted to drink. On the contrary. They are a very moral and sober race. They cater for the seafaring fraternity and take advantage of the simple and childish minds of sailor men to supply them with bad drink and hire a few painted hags to act as decoys and wheedle expensive drinks out of Jack, while the suave and smiling proprietors reap a golden harvest. The majority of these houses are as low as any to be found in the Ratcliffe Highway or Chatham Brook, but one particular house I visited required the purchase of a sixpenny ticket which made it what would be called in England - select. This house had some pretence to being called a music hall, but the only differences I could see were that the women were more showy and under dressed than their sisters in the more common houses, the drinks were more expensive and the patrons for the most part were young bloods from the Navy; officers and gentlemen(?) (By Act of Parliament).*

*There is a part of the town wholly given over to prostitution, and the human wreckage drifted there, mostly from the southern countries of Europe earning good trade whenever leave is granted from the ships. Of course Malta does not differ in this respect from any other town in the Mediterranean or in fact from any town in the world, but here it is recognised* *and no mistakes can be made as I have seen in England where respectable women are accosted by mistake and unpleasantness is often the result. The prostitutes here live apart and are medically examined periodically, and have a regular scale of charging and one feels no more embarrassed when going to brine down (*Naval slang for "bedding down"?) *than one would feel in going to one's barber or shoemaker.*

The normalization of prostitution he describes seems a practical and sensible solution to an intractable problem to me – and surprising in a country which is so devoutly Roman Catholic. I searched for the district grandfather describes but I did not find Valetta's seamy side. Strait Street, known by servicemen as "The Gut," runs parallel to Republic Street and has divested itself of the ever-open bars, brothels and dance halls which constituted the gut. They have disappeared. After all, the quality of the visitor is different—no more desperate, sex-starved single men of the world's navies; and no doubt the quality of life of the island has changed. For the human wreckage grandfather describes, one would have to go to other places. And indeed Toronto and London show more signs of human wreckage in the numbers of prostitutes, beggars, and drug addicts than I ever saw in Malta.

*The great industry in Malta as everyone knows is lace-making. There are no great factories as would be naturally conjured up by the word industry, the women doing the work in their own homes. The work is in no way a drudge as the maker is allowed free range of her artistic fancies and the consequence is an article that cannot be surpassed for beauty and*

52

*workmanship. Capitalism has not driven them into factories where they would develop into mere cogs in a gigantic machine and be sweated and robbed to boot to make profits for shareholders in London or elsewhere.*

*We proceeded to a bay just round the corner from Malta called St. Paul's Bay to work up for the annual Battle Practice. The Apostle Paul was supposed to have landed here and to commemorate the event a monument has been erected to his memory. He came to the bay with his glorious gospel of peace; we came to practice for war; truly if a tree be known by its fruit then the Christian religion has nothing to boast about in the matter of progress. However, we managed to pave a part of the bottom of this bay with shells of divers sizes and returned to Malta on Thursday; leave being granted as usual.*

*The real firing was to come off on the following week and to make sure that there would be as few fatheads as possible we left Malta on Saturday and anchored at a God-forgotten place called Bougi-Bougi. Leave was granted on Sunday afternoon and along with a few messmates I went ashore. We found a cabman willing to take us to Malta and off we went and after an hour's drive through a rather barren country, eventually arrived at the Sergeants' mess of the Argyle and Sutherland Highlanders. We spent a few hours with the members playing snap and sampling their beer which, by the way, came from Scotland, and then after a doch-an-doris we climbed into our cab and had a most enjoyable moonlight drive back to Bougi-Bougi.*

*The Battle Practice occupied the biggest part of a week and when our show came off we got two hits on the target just*

*beating the Suffolk by half a hit. After this brilliant*
*performance we returned to harbour and stayed until the end*
*of October.*


At the Valetta terminus I boarded a rattly Leyland diesel bus bound for St Paul's Bay. It deposited me on the bayside boulevard outside a McDogfoods restaurant, which I carefully skirted and had breakfast instead at a Maltese establishment with the fine full sweep of the bay before me. Once I had consulted my map and the waiter, I had my bearings and realized that I was eating my traditional sausage, egg and toast at the juncture of the old fishing village of St Paul's and the garish holiday resort of Bugibba. The rocky barren shore grandfather describes as "Buggi-Buggi" has become a sea of upscale high rise apartments, hotels, a casino and an endless strip of neon cafes, bingos, and fish-and-chip stands. Still God-forgotten, though.

After my ample breakfast, I decided to explore Bugibba first. The busy road which hugs the bay has a beautifully tiled pedestrian walkway on the ocean side; perfect for the aging couples out for a stroll as well as the local teenagers passing a football to and fro as they made their way to the beach for a game. The action was on the opposite pavement: window shoppers and sightseers jostling each other along - and the holiday season was not due for another three weeks. Grandfather would be amazed at the change, which has occurred since Bugibba was "discovered" in the 1970's and 80's by Maltese speculators with what my guidebook describes as "heady recklessness." Bewitched by the lucrative earnings of early tourism they erected multistory apartment buildings and hotels with no thought for aesthetics or planned development. The central pedestrian-only square and the palm-lined pavements represent belated attempts to impose order on chaos. The main street, aptly named Triq It-Turisti or Tourist Street, is a mass of cars, hawkers and touts offering trips and trinkets galore. A far cry from the barren shore and occasional horse-drawn garries of my grandfather's time.

Suddenly the tarmac ended and so did the high rises; but the presence of a construction crane indicated that a second tier was being developed. I headed back towards the old buildings and the quiet little harbour of St Paul's Bay. There is still a fishing fleet based here although pleasure craft crowd out the anchorages. At the turn of the last century, according to my trusty guidebook, just 200 people inhabited this quiet fishing port, best known as the place where St Paul's ship ran aground in 60 AD. The saint has a special place in Maltese hearts for having repaid their hospitality by removing the venom from the local snake population. The Maltese population is 99% staunchly Roman Catholic and 70% attend Mass every Sunday. A guide revealed that most of the older people go to mass every day. So grandfather's glimpse of tiny, rising cloud of socialism has not shaken the islanders' faith, despite being under a Labour government led by the fiery anti-Catholic Premier, Dom Mintoff, for most of the years after British rule ended in 1966.

I found the Shipwreck Church quiet and, thankfully, without tourists after the flurry of Bugibba. The building is actually a reconstruction of the original 14th Century church with its 17th Century modifications, which was flattened by a WW2 bomb. Very plain stone situated on an elevated site above the waterfront, it has a simple interior with a Maltese

Cross carved on the altar. I think the plain-speaking Apostle would approve, especially of his portrait behind the altar with his hands raised up in supplication. Twisty streets and narrow alleyways give an authenticity to St Paul's so lacking in its gaudy neighbour. I found a tiny junk shop in a low row of shops adjacent to the church. Looking around I found a brass cartridge case to remind me of the shells fired by the Lancaster in the bay and a model of a dghaisa complete with miniature oars.

# CHAPTER 4: MALTA

*Forty-two hours general leave was granted to each watch and as usual the town was invaded by crowds of British Blues , some drinking, some strolling around, some besieging the shops in search of suitable presents for the loved ones at home and some parading down the Rag where the sawmills are situated in quest of legs to saw up. I did the same things as I saw others do, but time hangs heavy on one's hand in a foreign town when one has exhausted the sights and having done Malta pretty well I sought pastures new in the shape of an excursion to Citta Vechia. A friend, who had come ashore with me, accompanied me on this trip. We started from the British Modern Club after a hearty breakfast and, scorning cabs and tramways, we swung along the road to C.V. at a good four miles an hour. We had got about 2 miles along the road when a brigand in the shape of a guide appeared on the scene and, though he didn't hold us up and go through our pockets in the orthodox manner, before he parted from us he had extracted a fair amount of the root of evil from our slender purses. Apparently he had walked from Citta Vechia in the early hours of the morning and had made an ambush in a roadside inn and we happened to be the first victims to pass along the road.*

*He scorned boots and although the day was cold and wet he trotted along quite cheerfully, carrying his coat on his arm, and regaled us with snatches of the history of the Island of Malta. Every one who has been to C.V. knows that the Cathedral is one of the most historic in the world and it was to this holy place our brigand led us first. He had many accomplices in the town as we subsequently found to our sorrow. His duty apparently lay in leading us to the entrances of the interesting places we visited and then turning us over to one of his accomplished followers. The one in the Cathedral, however, was a rather decent fellow and spoke very good English and on the whole was worth the shilling he demanded.*

*As it was nearing Christmas, many of the gold and silver ornaments were on view and the walls were festooned with gay silk cloth manufactured in Lyons. The most interesting sight is an original (?) painting of St. Paul executed by a Greek artist. The painting, with the exception of the face, hands and feet, is covered over with a silver replica and this replica is only swung back when distinguished visitors come to the Cathedral and our guide assured us that the last time the painting was fully exposed was when the late King Edward VII visited the Island a few years ago.*

*The monarch of England is specially catered for in this edifice as he enjoys, along with the Archbishop of Malta, a special chair on a raised dais near the grand altar, and no-one, so our guide told us, has ever placed his or her backside on this beautiful seat except the reigning Monarch. I could not help thinking and wondering if the late Monarch has a reserved seat among the angels or if his spirit is wandering among the dark places searching for a special chair for its bum (that is if spirits have bums) and finding none. But my fancy was not allowed to run long in this train as the guide led us under the dome and directing our eyes upwards we were amazed and delighted with the beauty and splendour of the paintings and frescoes that covered the interior of this vast structure. I like paintings or rather I like bright colors and I wish the walls of all houses were covered with paintings as nice as the ones we saw on the inside of this Cathedral.*

Citta Vecchia (Old City) was the name given by the Knights of Malta to the original capital of Malta after they had built Valetta and moved the capital to its new site there in 1571. However, the Maltese prefer to call it by its Arabic name, Mdina. Although grandfather does not mention it, the city was heavily fortified with walls by the Knights of Malta to protect it from invasion by the Turks. Palaces, a Cathedral (which he does describe), monasteries, museums, public buildings and residences are all contained within the confines of the walls which are still intact. In bright sunny weather a number of us were picnicking on their wide expanse. For many years the ancient city has been known as the Silent City, for the streets are too narrow for vehicle traffic and the tall buildings and solid walls cut the noise even of the throngs of tourists peopling the laneways. Approaching on the bus I could see both Mdina and the adjoining town of Rabat from miles away as they stand on a high ridge. Over the centuries Mdina's location has made it easy to defend; in 1429, so legend has it, St Paul appeared on a white charger with flaming sword and helped put the invading Saracens to rout.

On emerging from this splendid Cathedral, we were seized upon by our guide and led to the entrance of the "Grotto of St. Paul." We were handed over to another accomplice, who unlocked the gates and by the aid of candles lighted us down the steps to the Grotto. We saw the altar erected to the memory of St. Paul on the spot where the first Christian church was instituted and where mass is said every day for the peace of his soul. [The guide ]next led us into the cave where Paul and his shipwrecked comrades lived for a time, and in this cave is a splendid marble statue of the Apostle. Numerous little knick-knacks in the shapes of saints bones and ancient books were trotted out for our inspection but bones, saints, or otherwise unless they have meat on, do not appeal to me.

We had to pay up and look pleasant for these privileges. Oh Paul! otherwise Saul why did you choose the Island of Malta to get wrecked upon? It will soon be a choice between following your career a little further or going short of beer. However our guide next led us to the entrance of the catacombs or cemetery of St. Agatha. We were as per routine handed over to the inevitable accomplice and the latter lighting two candles unlocked the iron wicket which guards the entrance and preceded us down the steps leading to these marvellous underground dwellings of the dead. We learned from our guide that the Phoenicians were the people who had lived here and made the wonderful underground city. Though the principal passages have been closed up, owing to insufficient ventilation, there remains enough to interest the visitor. These people had lived on one side of their underground house and, when they handed in their checks, were buried on the other side. Their beds were hewn from the solid rock and though there are many stories about those ancient gents and their Mormon ideas, we could find no trace *where it could have been possible to squeeze in two damsels beside one man.*

*That they know what they were there for was quite evident, as there were numerous graves of infants in the walls and floors. We emerged at a different point than that which we had entered and found our original guide grinning at the entrance. He took us next to a Maltese Inn and ordered tea for us, after which he gave us to understand that the day being for spent and the evening near at hand and the next train left for Malta in twenty minutes time, that he would deem it a favour if we would in Naval parlance "divvy up." The usual altercation took place; he demanding a higher fee than we were prepared to pay, but we eventually arrived at a settlement, and just to square the deal he drank the remains of our tea and ate the remains of our banquet, and smiling, scraping and with many "Good day Sahibs" he took his departure and no doubt found some other victim to exercise his charms upon before the night was out.*

*We repaired to the railway station and boarded the train for Valetta, where we arrived about five o'clock in the evening, having spent a most enjoyable day.*


Rabat (from the Arab name for suburb) adjoins Mdina and forms its commercial centre with banks, offices, shops and restaurants. Before the fortifications were built the two cities formed a single community; now they have reunited again. However Rabat is far from silent. It is a brash neighbour, abounding in tourist trinket shops and hole–in-the- wall pubs. The most prominent feature - apart from St Paul's Church at the heart of the community - are the catacombs, which run for miles under the town. These were a maze of early Christian burial chambers originally excavated in the 4$^{th}$ and 5$^{th}$ centuries, covered up, and then rediscovered in 1894. Grandfather describes both the Church and the catacombs which he explored with the help of the guide's lantern. Nowadays you pick up an earpiece with commentary in the language of your choice from the kiosk and take a self-guided tour through the labyrinth. Once I got used to hunching down under the low ceilings in the narrow passages and to the low light I found it a quieting experience. I gazed down at the bed-like tombs cut from the rough, stone walls, some of which were child-sized. Some receded far up narrow alcoves and niches. At intervals alongside the gravesites were agape tables and benches cut out of the rock for families to pray and feast in honour of their loved ones. Feasting together with the dead relatives was a sound practice for families, I thought. Children would become familiar with notions of death and treat it as a natural event. Perhaps grandfather would have approved. A larger open area connected with the tombs served as an underground place of worship during times of persecution. Unfortunately St Agatha's catacombs with the frescoes and remains were not open at the time I visited.

*We were in Malta now for a long spell and in consequence had plenty of time for a good many tours round the Island of Malta. I propose here to deal with several things relating to Malta and Maltese life that might be both useful and instructive to my readers. It is justly claimed for the Maltese Islands that equality of temperature is a prominent characteristic. Twenty degrees - between 50 degrees and 70 degrees - may be taken as the full range of shade temperature during 2/3 of the year, the cool season; while a maximum of 90 degrees and a minimum of 70 degrees hold during the four* summer months, June to September. The average shade temperature throughout the year is 64 degrees. In summer time it is a common sight to see the poorer classes, who enjoy good health and often live to a great age, sleeping outdoors at night. The peasantry are particularly robust and vigorous.

The prevailing winds are from the north-west and south-east. The former predominates and is bracing and invigorating. The south-east wind, known locally as the "Sirocco," coming mostly in September but often in other seasons, is not a welcome visitor. Many people, both English and natives, experience languor and depression, although others seem to be insensible to its influence. Proceeding from the deserts of Africa, and becoming heavily charged with vapour in its passage across a considerable expanse of sea, the "Sirocco" arrives in Malta, close, damp, and misty causing not a little discomfort. Whether it deserves all the hard things said about it is open to question. The mean quantity of moisture in the air of the Mediterranean basin is about one half of that in the atmosphere of England.

The behaviour of the north-east wind offers a variety not less unwelcome. Its visits in full virulence are happily rare, but at such times the sea casts a picturesque smother over the jutting points of St. Elmo, Ricasoli, and Tigne, and, despite the protection of the breakwaters at the Grand Harbour entrance, churns up the surface of harbours and creeks, incidentally providing scope for the magnificent prowess and skill of the boatmen who ply for hire on these waters. The hardy oarsmen, descendants of those who won sea battles of the Grand Masters, seem well able to deal with the stormy conditions even after steam launch navigation is temporarily suspended. Watch them with a north-easter in full force, two men to a "Dghaisa", with a passenger. With a *graceful sweep of the heavy but well balanced oar, the boat is urged along. As successive rollers, warily watched and met direct prow on, are "jumped" in perfect safety, one realises that this is expert rowing by the finest exponents in the world. With his stout craft thus under complete control, "Jose" has no fears in the pursuit of his business nor need the passenger have any misgivings, for accidents are almost unknown when "Salt-fish", "Michael", or other prominent boatmen take charge.*

*The Maltese are a hardy, frugal and industrious race. The peasantry, which comprises the bulk of the population, appears to have found it possible to rear large and healthy families and to thrive on the "irreducible minimum". To realise this, one has to grasp the fact that bare food of the cheapest description, scanty clothing, and a boxlike house for a dwelling, will still build up a sturdy constitution under healthy conditions of life spent in open-air occupations. A Chinese coolie is better housed and fed than the Maltese countryman, and an English labourer is luxuriously served in both respects in comparison, but neither can boast of bodily strength and vigour such as is possessed by the average Maltese peasant.*

*Education has, during recent years, been placed within the reach of the poorest boy and girl, and this has helped to cultivate the business aptitude ingrafted in the native character. In the matter of driving a bargain with these shrewd islanders you will need to exercise all your wits if the transaction is to be in your favour. It is obviously quite futile to cast the blame on "Jose", thus naturally gifted with business acumen, when in a fair and square deal he gets the advantage. No Jew, it is said, can live in Malta. One must not, however, conclude that the truth of the statement reflects discredit on the Maltese; we often hear the saying, "It takes seven Jews to cheat one Maltese."*

*The history of Malta would require a volume for itself and is far beyond the scope of this humble scribe but I shall give the historical date from reliable authority as it might prove interesting.*

*The Phoenicians occupied the island about 1500 B.C.*

*Greeks 700*

*Carthaginians 480*

*Romans 216*

*Arabs 870 A.D.*

*Normans 1090*

*The island then passed successively to Germany, France, and Spain. In 1530 it was granted by Charles V to the Knights of St. John of Jerusalem who held sway for 268 years.*

Grandfather's sources for the history of Malta were, of course, limited to what was known in 1910. Now we know that the Phoenicians did not arrive in Malta until 800 BC. They would have found at least the remnants of the Bronze Age inhabitants who preceded them and lived in one-roomed cottages called dolmens which can still be seen. It has been established that they invaded Malta from the North around 2300 BC. They used the temples (such as those in the Tarxien complex) built by their Neolithic predecessors as crematoria and places for elaborate funeral rites. The first known settlers emigrated from Sicily in about 5000 BC bringing with them seeds and livestock. At first, they lived in caves and cleared land for farming. Five hundred years later they started living in huts built of stone, clay and twigs. Traces of these hamlets survive together with evidence that they worshipped fertility goddesses. None of their prehistoric artifacts or information about them would have been known a hundred years ago, for they lay under the ground waiting for the pioneering archaeologist, Sir Themistocles Zammit, to unearth and identify them.

Grandfather's history of Malta ends with the Knights of St. John ceding power to a French force under Napoleon in 1798. The French were soon after defeated by the British in 1800; the British occupation lasted in different forms until 1964, when the Maltese finally gained independence.

I discovered the origins of the local language, Malti: it is derived from spoken Phoenician and has undergone 2000 years of addition and development. From the 9th Century on, many Arabic words from the invaders were adopted into Malti since both languages shared Semitic roots. The languages of subsequent invaders likewise influenced the language of the Maltese. A written form was developed in the 18th and 19th centuries after many years of oral transmission. Unlike Arabic, Malti uses Latin characters. In 1964 it became the official language of Malta with English still a strong second. Both are taught in school together with Italian and French.

*There are a great many interesting sights and objects of historical interest in and around Valetta but there is one to which I wish to make special reference as it appears to be a matter of speculation as to where it is situated and what is to be seen when found. I am referring to what is called by the uninitiated "Underground Malta". What this really means is a slum, not underground but hidden away in a hollow and known as the Manderaggio. It is reputed to be the most crowded locality in the world, and may be described as a deep basin bounded by the high back walls of the houses on four surrounding streets in quadrilateral form. In area it covers about 2 ½ acres. Hundreds of small houses are built on the slopes of the cavity; from the three entrances a narrow, winding and rather complicated route descends to the bottom by flights of steps. Within the Manderaggio is massed a population of probably not less than 3000 people, many being market people who are better off than one might suppose. The conditions may not be all that could be wished, but in point of cleanliness (or dirtiness) I should say the place compares favourably with the dwellings of the poorer classes elsewhere on the island.*

*Much has appeared in English papers as to the Manderaggio being unsafe for visitors and the lawlessness of its occupants. This was certainly not my experience: a guide is advisable, owing to the complicated alleys, otherwise one need have no scruples in visiting this remarkable spot. The entrance near Marsamuscetto steps, in Strada San Marco is perhaps the most convenient point of access. Another place worth a visit is the "Chapel of Bones". This is a weird collection of human bones artistically arranged in a vault under the soldiers Club at the lower end of Strada Mercanti. Those who have seen the collections in Hythe Church crypt in Kent, and other parts of England will admit that the design, though ghastly, is rather curious and novel notwithstanding.*

*ject of churches I might mention that anyone*
*choice of at least twenty in Valetta and every*
*sit.*

While in Valetta I made several unsuccessful efforts to find this area: the Manderaggio slum with its macabre Chapel of Bones. Only after my return home with the help of my local library did I discover the reason for my failure – it ceased to exist in the 1950's. The slum was torn down and replaced by blocks of social housing and tenements for the workers. The irony is that the ferry from Sliema (and our hotel) crosses the Marsamxett Harbour and lands in Valetta at one corner of the old slum district! So each time we crossed to explore Valetta my companion Jay and I would walk up to the city centre through the old Manderaggio district.

The story behind the slum is interesting: Valetta was built as a fortified city by the Knights of Malta in the 16th Century after the first Great Siege of Malta by the Turkish Army under Suleiman the Magnificent. The attack failed. By the time additions were made a century later Valetta could house 40,000 people with all their needs within the walls. It was and still remains one of the most heavily fortified cities in the world and served as a model for other walled cities such as Kingston, Jamaica and London after the Great Fire. However the Manderaggio district is a monument to the one miscalculation made by the Knights; they wanted a port on the Marsamxett harbour hewn out of the rock on the north side of Valetta. The harbour proved to provide less shelter from the weather than the Grand Harbour on the opposite side so they abandoned the project leaving a quarry. Poor families soon created crude dwellings for themselves in the hollow, resulting in a sordid and overcrowded slum. By the time of British rule in the 1880's 2544 people lived in its 2.56 acres. Mr. Plimsoll, an English M.P., was shocked at the living conditions of the inhabitants and wrote a pamphlet for his fellow parliamentarians which eventually led to new housing projects. Evelyn Waugh, who visited Valetta in the 1920's, was too scared to venture there after dark and described it as "the most concentrated slum in the world." Echoes of grandfather!

The population of Valetta has decreased from about 25,000 in the late 1800's to 7,200 today, because of the closure of the British military bases in 1979 and because people have moved out to the spacious surrounding towns.

*We went into dry dock to have our bottom scraped and underwater fittings attended to. The weather was supposed to be very cold for Malta and I might add that up to and including Easter week the weather remained cold and cheerless with abundance of rain, and for the time of the year one might just as well have been in dismal England. I was much taken up with the way the Easter or Holy week was spent in Malta. From Wednesday afternoon a representation of the Lord's Supper was on view in the Chapel of the convent adjoining St. Dominic's church in Valetta. This was a most striking and impressive illustration of the greatest event in the life of Jesus and had special interest for those who had not previously witnessed it. The meal, comprised bread in the form of small loaves, circular cakes, paste and sweet stuff shaped as fish and was so dispositioned and apportioned as to indicate the places occupied at the table by the apostles and their divine master. There were a great many spectators filing* round the table while I was there and I learned that all the food was collected on the following morning and given to the poor. On Maundy Thursday, His Grace the Archbishop of Malta officiated at High Mass in the Co-Cathedral of St. John, where the ceremony of the consecration of the Holy Oils was performed, also that of washing the feet of the apostles in which latter office His Grace testifies in person to the humility of the head of the church. The Rome ceremony is carried out in the English Church, I believe; the bishop picking out twelve of the nicest looking choir boys and washing their feet. I am open to correction here as I am rather ignorant of the pagan acts and rituals of the worlds' religions.

The morning services and ceremonies commenced at nine, upon the conclusion of which the bells of the Island Churches were silenced and nothing was heard but the weird striking of the clocks, and the occasional rattle of wooden clappers erected in the belfries, intended, I think, to illustrate the rending of the veil of the temple. On this day the repository sepulchres were exposed to worshippers. The several churches vie in the preparation of these striking representations, the sarcophagi and other allegorical devices being enveloped in a profusion of candles and dressed with flowers, plants and exotics. The faithful are expected to visit seven churches during the day or on the following morning, in remembrance of the seven last words of our Saviour. During this time the city was practically silent, the people singly and in parties, dressed in sombre attire, passed to and from the churches, reciting prayers on the way, with numerous processions of the several religious congregations attired in the dress of their respective orders, making up a scene which seemed to impress the natives to an overwhelming degree.

70

*On Good Friday, the ceremony of the Adoration of the Cross takes place in all the churches of the Island, following Mass of the Presanctified, at 9.00 a.m. The proceedings at the Co-Cathedral of St. John, Valetta, are of a very imposing and impressive character. His Grace the Archbishop officiates. At 5-30 the famous procession of the Passion leaves the Church of Jesus on Strada San Giovanni Steps, Valetta. The several events leading up to the Crucifixion and the descent from the Cross are faithfully depicted. The nobility and gentry are not infrequently included among the hooded and surpliced bearers of the statues and tableaux, it being customary to make the occasion one of atonement and humiliation.*

*On Saturday morning, the Ceremony of Blessing the Font takes place in the Co-Cathedral and all churches. Pontifical mass is celebrated about 9.00 and the "Gloria in Excelsis Deo" is sung, at the conclusion of which, and at the signal given by the co-Cathedral, the bells which had been silenced since Thursday, resume their function in a simultaneous peal, where upon the drapery enveloping the interior of the churches is removed, light is let in in welcome gleams from the uncovered windows, while in the streets bands play merrily and the people give way to rejoicing and congratulations.*

*On Easter Sunday morning at dawn, a very quaint and interesting ceremony takes place. A statue of "Christ risen" is taken from the Greek Church, Strada Vercous, near the Valetta Palace, and carried up to the Barracca. Thence it is borne down by Strada Mercanti to the Granaries, St. Elmo, and afterwards brought to the bottom of Strada Reale, whence, at a given signal it is dragged up the ascent by means of ropes at the utmost speed obtainable amid the shouts and plandits of the multitude, the whole forming what is used to*

71

*describe some comic film in a Maltese cinematography namely "A comic scene of great hilarity" or the "Ne plus ultra of comic scenes" as I saw one enterprising Maltese describe his show.*

*We spent over a month in dry dock thoroughly cleaning and painting the bottom, shipping spare propeller blades, etc. We had a trial on the following Thursday and, as the machinery was considered satisfactory, we returned to Bighi Bay in Valetta and tied up to our buoy the same afternoon.*

After spending a hectic week in Valetta, where tourists and traffic spill over the winding medieval streets, Jay and I escaped to the tiny island of Gozo which is north of the main island but still administratively part of Malta. The apartment was in Xlendi, a quiet holiday village with a fishing port. It is tucked into a fiord-like ravine of massive rocks which enclose the hotels and apartment blocks so tightly on each side that the cliffs appear to form their back walls. I gazed out of the plate glass windows at the grey, craggy landscape and the crashing waves reflecting on the warmth and helpfulness of the Maltese and Gozitans we had met during our stay: taxi drivers, bus drivers, wait staff, tour operators, shop owners and casual information givers on the street. We have had longer encounters with a few people: George conducted us on a personal six-hour tour round the sights of Gozo: he was most informative about the history and significance of what we saw. On a walk through Gozo's main town, Victoria, we discovered the Astra Opera House which stood like a lone tooth in a decaying mouth next to vacant lots on the main street. We wandered in to explore its fading elegance and chanced to meet another George backstage. George is a popular name in Malta because the island was awarded the George Cross by Britain for the bravery of its citizens during the second World War This George was a volunteer in the theatre's costumes and props department and gave us an impromptu tour with a history of the once thriving theatre. Although it stages fewer theatre productions today, it hosts a gala production with top international opera stars each year. I liked the baroque interior with ornate boxes and balconies even though neglect had taken its toll. George showed us photographs of various projects and stars he had worked with. He allowed us to try on masks and showed us costumes he had made. Then there was Emanuel, with whom we hitched a ride from Victoria to Xlendi in a car with a Maple Leaf insignia on the rear window. He had come back to Xlendi after living in Toronto for 28 years and was a recovering alcoholic. He was open about his struggle and told us details about his family and their island history.

Jay's feet were cold after our tour of the windy Citadel in Victoria. By chance we met up with a man called Charlie in the market. He told us that he owned a small clothing store which was closed for the siesta. However, when he heard that Jay's feet were cold, Charlie insisted on opening his shop and sold her a pair of socks. He then spoofed at auctioning her body to passers by with the bidding opening at fifty pounds! Later during the walk I spied a barber's shop which reminded me that I needed my eyebrows trimmed. As I grow older, hair seems to migrate from its regular places on my body to sprout outrageously elsewhere. I walked into the shop where animated conversations broke off when the owner asked me how he could help. I explained and, while I stood in front of him, he trimmed the recalcitrant hair into line with his swift-clicking scissors. "No problem" - and no charge.

From these and other encounters, I have concluded that the inhabitants of Malta are a kind and generous people. Perhaps it is their long history of being oppressed, their experience of the different cultures of their oppressors or the kinship bonds they have in a relatively small country (400,000 inhabitants) that have fostered this sense of community.

The prehistoric sites have given me feelings of awe and wonder. These were especially strong as I stood inside one of the temples at Ggantija on Gozo. Immense       stones were believed to have been brought here by giants (hence the name) from a valley some distance away. These temples are the oldest free-standing structures in the world. I closed my eyes facing the altar and slow vibrations gradually spread up from my legs to my chest and my belly until my whole body felt alive with them. I was overcome with emotion, a strange mix of excitement and peace. It was like a homecoming as I imagined looking up at the colossal statue of the Goddess which had once towered over the enclosed space.

Visits to other historic sites revealed further riches of Maltese culture. A cave, reputed to be that of Calypso, who held Odysseus captive for seven years, overlooks a sandy beach and a grove resembling an earthly paradise. At M'dina, outside the walled fortress built to ward off the Arabs and the Corsairs from North Africa, there stand the remains of a Roman town house with exquisite mosaic floors, glass vessels, pottery and marble statues; a monument to the achievements of the patriarchal culture that followed the ancient matriarchal one.

On the day of our departure from Gozo the van from Xlendi Tourist Services called for us at 6 am to drive us to the ferry for the mainland. They had arranged for a second van to take us from the ferry terminal on the main island to the airport 14 miles away in time for our London flight at 10 am. We were dropped off with time to spare to board the waiting ferry. As I stepped down from the van I realized I was not sure where I had put the airline tickets and my passport. I searched everywhere. Horrors! I remembered that I had left them in a drawer at the apartment 10 kilometers away. The driver had left and we had 20 minutes before the ferry sailed.

"We'll make the plane," Jay said.

I explained the dire circumstances to a police officer who had greeted us warmly as we arrived.

"I am so stupid."

"No you are not", he said; "Such things happen all the time. Besides, much better it happens at the end and not the beginning of your holiday. No problem; we will phone and get George to drive them here. If you miss the ferry there is another in 45 minutes which will get you to your plane."

He and I walked swiftly to his office across the harbour and roused George's son from his bed. I explained, apologetically. "No problem; wait for me at the gate." With five minutes to go and no sign of rescue, the helpful police officer shook his head: "Next boat." Then: screeching tires, a swift handshake and we made the ferry with two minutes to spare. I looked into the friendly police officer's eyes as I thanked him and said farewell. And strangely, I thought his eyes turned from brown to a familiar blue; his face wrinkled and crinkled with laugh lines.

"Grandfather," I said, "in Gibraltar you did say you would keep an eye on me in my travels." I wondered if Jay heard me. She certainly didn't hear his reply.

"Laddie, I am in your footsteps all the way; dinna fash yerself on my account now."

He solemnly winked at me as his face reverted to that of the friendly police officer: "Sahha," he said, "as we say goodbye in our Malti language."

Safe on the ferry, I mulled over the incident. The police officer had responded to my calling myself "stupid" for forgetting the tickets by reassuring me that I was not stupid, that he had encountered many others who had done the same and then given me the information that a second ferry would depart in sufficient time for me to catch the flight. His compassionate response made me realize how often I make harsh judgments of myself over my shortcomings. Further, I tend to rely on my memory when planning trips rather than make written checklists of the things I have to do. As I grow older my memory has lapses so I need to list and check off my "to-do's" more carefully It occurred to me that, not only am I discovering my grandfather through following his travels, he is helping me discover myself and teaching me lessons in life.

# CHAPTER 5: EGYPT

## CAIRO

Jay and I flew into Cairo and took a taxi to the Nile Hilton hotel. My first impressions of Cairo were of blinding sunlight and police all over the airport dressed in black fatigues and black berets toting machine guns. The taxi trip was hair-raising - around us a melee of cars, trucks and buses, and pedestrians darting across the roads. The air was full of screeching horns and squealing brakes; there were no traffic lanes, cars simply rushing and slithering past each other. Our driver spoke good English and gave us a commentary on the buildings we passed, the percentage of Christians and Muslims in Cairo and the city's population (23 million); all this between cell phone calls, his hands alternately off and on the steering wheel.

Funnily enough my grandfather also complained about the traffic in Cairo 100 years ago. In his case he was dodging donkey carts and horses. He arrived in the city by train from Alexandria, where HMS Lancaster had docked.

*There was an invitation sent from the Scots Guards, who were stationed at Cairo, for a party from each ship to visit them for three days. I formed one of the party from our ship and taken altogether it was by far the most enjoyable and interesting tour that has fallen to my lot to be present at. The distance from Alexandria to Cairo is 128 miles and the Egyptian State Railway took us in a 2$^{nd}$ class coach from the landing stage to Cairo for the sum of 4 and 9 pence return fare. (No dividends* *for profit mongers). The scenery all the way to Cairo is typical of an English county except the native dresses and un-English faces. The Valley of the Nile is remarkably fertile and by a system of irrigation three crops a year can be obtained. Cotton, wheat and other cereals, trefoil and potatoes are the principal crops and in some places rice is grown. The methods employed in watering the crops are very primitive and when one sees them first ones' mind harks back to pictures depicting Eastern scenes in the old family Bibles. A rough wooden wheel with buckets or jars attached round the circumference rotated by a wooden cog wheel which is turned either by oxen or camel, lifts the water from the Nile or its tributaries and pours it into a canal from whence it is diverted through numerous channels to the roots of the various crops.*

*I saw an even more primitive method than this employed on some of the smaller farms. An upright post carrying a cross bar pivoted in the centre and having at one end a bucket on a string and at the other end a counterbalance, in the shape of a big stone, comprised a rough and ready means of irrigation. The modus operandi was simple, the man or woman simply pulling down on the bucket end until it dipped in the water and then releasing their hold, the weight took charge and lifted the bucket to the level of the canal where it was emptied by an attendant and then returned to the Nile again and recharged.*

Grandfather and I had the same priority on our arrival: we were both determined to see the pyramids and the sphinx at Giza on the outskirts of Cairo. In 1962, Caroline (my first wife) and I flew into Cairo on a four day flight from Johannesburg to London run by a firm called Trek Airways. Jets were being phased in and Trek offered a cut-rate alternative using propeller-driven aircraft from the previous era. This was a leisurely experience as the Constellations only flew by day, giving passengers the late afternoon and evening to explore each stopover city and luxurious hotel accommodation for the night. Caroline and I dropped off our luggage at the Nile Hilton Hotel and piled on to a coach into the desert. We were met by camels whose owners chanted as they made a beeline for the fresh load of tourists: "The camels are coming, hooray, hooray!" And we were in the thick of bargaining, gawping and camel riding. In 2010 I found the facilities considerably altered. The monuments rose out of the pale sand as always but there were lines of stalls with wares and owners spread out alongside the familiar sites. Huge banks of chairs for those who watch the spectacular son-e-lumiere light show after dark. Various tour agencies and cafes dot the walk from the parking areas. One vendor amongst a throng asked:

"Where you from?"

"Canada"

"Oh Canada Dry" (guffaw) "Welcome in Egypt!"

I did feel their welcome too, even from those who pressured me to buy their trinkets, their minute packs of Kleenex or their guidebooks. When they followed me down the street getting more and more persistent I discovered a perfect stopper. I would bow with my hands clasped and say "Salaam alaikum" (Peace be with you), to which there is a formulaic reply: "Wa alaikum salaam" (And peace to you.) This ritual would silence them and they just give up their pestering! Hotel and restaurant staff were courteous and helpful; people on the street who heard me trying to get directions or ask for bus tickets would translate. In one case a man who had helped with tickets and directions kept an eye on us until Jay and I boarded the bus, making sure that we went to the right platform at the right time. I discovered that there is a dignity and a set of manners among the Arabs and that one can go beyond the superficial by simply offering friendship and respect.

Here is Grandfather's account of his visit to the pyramids:

*We arrived in Cairo about mid-day and were immediately taken charge of by the Sergeants of the Guards who took us to their mess at the Kasr-el-Nil Barracks and copiously irrigated us with good beer and whisky and afterwards we dined in style on a good old Scotch dinner. A party was at once formed to visit the Pyramids and Sphinx and about 2 o'clock we set off on cars, and about 3/4 of an hours run brought us almost to the base of the Great Pyramid of Cheops. The Pyramids were built about 4,235 years B.C. and were tombs of ancient Kings. The height of the first pyramid is 481 feet and by climbing to the top an excellent view of the Nile Delta can be obtained. I do not intend to describe the pyramids in detail as so much has been written about them that it would be superfluous on my part to try and add anything to what has already been compiled. Suffice for me to say that a visit in person does much to knock the romance that is attached to them on the head and one comes away with much the same feeling that one gets when he has been had in a side show at a circus.*

I did not feel ripped off as grandfather did on either of my two visits to the Pyramids. From the city they look like small one dimensional triangles through the shimmering haze of pollution but as I walked up closer I felt elated at their size and sheer splendour. The second time my experience aroused a more spiritual sense in me. These were the largest structures on earth built as monuments to death and the certainty of an afterlife. The circus-like crowds of hawkers, camel drivers, guides and tourists did not detract from my feelings of awe and wonder. The lofty sphinx and I seemed to share a sardonic grin at the hordes below snapping away with their cameras or cell phones. I was also better-informed about how the pyramids were constructed. I had accepted the popular Hollywood explanation that hordes of slaves under whip-cracking overseers had been dragooned into hard labour. According to Andrew Beattie in his 2005 volume, *Cairo: a Cultural and Literary History*, recent evidence shows that the workers were farmers who were unable to work their fields flooded every summer by the waters of the Nile. They were housed during their annual make work project in nearby compounds and the flood provided them with a means to float heavy stones and other material to the work site. Mud from the flood enabled them to slide the huge blocks up to the next level of the growing pyramid.

After both visits I returned to the Nile Hilton Hotel overnight. This was the hotel Trek Airways booked for our second night out from Johannesburg. . I had such clear memories of ochre stone corridors, iced water taps and the stupendous view over the Nile that I booked in for a nostalgic visit. The same muffled cacophony of traffic sounds and chants still filtered through the balcony doors. The hotel has been owned for the last year by the Ritz Carlton group, a waiter told me. (I thought he said "Red Skeleton") It will close for 2 years from Dec 31, 2010 for a complete renovation. The staff will be paid a skeleton salary as a retainer – no tips, not happy.

I searched guide books, guides and street signs for the Kasr-el-Nil barracks McKay mentions at the beginning of the previous excerpt. On a whim I asked the elderly concierge at the hotel where the Kasr-el-Nil barracks might have been. He told me that there was a British barracks on the site of the Nile Hilton until the British army moved it to Port Said after Anthony Eden's misadventure over the Suez Canal. The hotel was opened by President Nasser in 1959. So I had been sleeping on Grandfather's favourite drinking spot in 1962 and again in 2009. The other interesting coincidence is that Sally, a character in *"The Mistress of Nothing"* (which I had just read), worked at the Nile Hotel after leaving Lady Duff Gordon in the 1860's.

Grandfather discovered, to his evident surprise, that a military parade could arouse his own bloodthirsty impulses:

*The next morning was Coronation day and the troops in the garrison paraded in full strength. The lines of troops formed three sides of a square, the Royal Horse Artillery occupying a position on the extreme right, next to them the 21$^{st}$ Lancers and Royal Engineers, and then the 1$^{st}$ Battalion of the Scots Guards, the 1$^{st}$ Battalion of the Rifle Brigade. The massed bands and pipes were formed up in front of the Royal Horse Artillery and Cavalry. The stand which stood at the rear of the Saluting base was soon filled with a motley and eager throng which was composed of every nationality in Cairo. Ministers, noted functionaries in the Government, the Diplomatic Corps of the foreign powers, civil and Military* *employees in the Egyptian State services, the elite of Cairo society both native and foreign, managers of banks and Commercial and Agricultural Sydicates and a vast crowd of civilian onlookers all found room in the seats laid out on the right and left of the grand stand.*

*At 7-55 a.m. the Regent, Mohammed Sais Pasha drove up to the place reserved for him, and was received with the Khedival Salute. Five minutes later, punctually at eight, the British Agent arrived and he too was received with a salute but this time it was the Royal Salute. The Coronation Parade then started. The picturesque ceremony of trooping the colours was first gone through, the various movements of the troops being carried out with faultless precision. As the sun's rays flashed from a drawn sword or a raised bayonet and as the eye travelled down the ranks of these picked troops one felt some prehistoric trait surging through his breast and filling him with a desire to kill somebody or something. The religious service came next and then the King was sung and five minutes afterwards the parade was dismissed, the whole ceremony lasting only about three quarters of an hour.*

*After the ceremonies were over we formed a party to visit the zoological gardens (another state institution by the way) and I must say I was agreeably surprised by the splendid condition of the lawns and walks. They are quite as good as the average English park which says a lot in a climate like this. The exhibits are nearly all African and I can say no more in praise of the gardens that they supply all the principal gardens in Europe from here. In the afternoon we attended the sports given by the military to the European residents in Cairo and here we had ample opportunity of criticising the hobble and the harem skirts as they were here in abundance. The sports were more for women and children and after a look*

83

*round the various amusements we had a nice donkey ride across the Nile bridge and home for tea. We were entertained to a smoking concert in the Sergeants mess in the evening and then to bed as we had a stiff day in front of us on the morrow.*

We visited the zoo and what I saw bore no resemblance to the tidy lawns and walks grandfather describes. The gravel paths remain but they are overgrown with weeds. The lawns are now bare patches covered with fallen branches and debris. I saw none of the rich tropical plants he describes. There are many sad-looking animals in small cages. I saw ibexes in a small paddock with a sign saying they can move at 65 KPH. Not in these cramped quarters. Some of the ruined buildings display their former grandeur; others are heaps of rubble. However many local people enjoy the spacious grounds and the shade provided by an abundance of trees even though it was a week day when I visited.

*We set off early the following morning to visit the Citadel, the highest point in Cairo. The citadel was built in 1135 AD by Mohamed Ali and was supposed to be impregnable until the great Napoleon shattered the popular belief (and incidentally the main gates) by a few well directed shells from his heavy cannon. As we passed through the battered gates we were amused at the inscription on an old chair which ran as follows- "No one except he who by the grace of God has lived for a hundred years may sit on this chair". No one in our party could lay claim to this distinction so we had no opportunity of finding out whether it was a comfortable seat or not. The various buildings inside the citadel are used for military stores and there is also a barracks here for a line regiment.*

*The Grand Mosque is inside the Citadel and is well worth a visit. It is quite modern as it was built as recently as 1896. According to the Mohammedan faith we had to put slippers over our boots before entering and remove them again when leaving the building. The first thing that struck us on entering was the entire absence of seats. The worshippers simply squat or kneel on the thick oriental carpet which covers the whole of the ground space. Here the Khedive worships when he is in residence in Cairo and he has a special entrance but no chair is provided for him. Inscribed round the dome in Arabic are the names of the Caliphs who were Minor Prophets to Mohamed.*

*On leaving the mosque we met with a Corporal in the Egyptian Army, a tubby good natured Englishman, who beamed on our party and jovially asked us to fall in and follow him. He led the way to what presumably was a grand palace but on entering we found it was the Sergeants mess of the Mounted Police. Our fat Corporal treated us to drinks all round and we blessed the fates that threw him across our path as climbing about in Cairo in mid-summer is dry work. He told us the building had once been the palace of an Egyptian who had walked in high places but now was unoccupied except the part used for the Sergeants mess. That this Egyptian had kept a harem was evident as the large marble bathroom was fitted with a seat and a round hole for the eunuch to keep his eye on the fair bathers. The smiling cheery, corporal looked through the hole and I think in his imagination he pictured the bath peopled with the fair sex, for he turned to us and said with a twinkle in his eye "Those old princes knew how to enjoy life and no doubt they found much pleasure in it."*

*He then took us to a window from which a splendid birds-eye view of the city and its environments could be obtained. In the distance could be seen the pyramids of Giza and then miles nearer the bigger and more famous ones we had visited. The great aqueduct, built by Napoleon to bring water from the Nile to the Citadel, twined away in the distance like a giant centipede. The city, with its mosques and minarets, and flat-roofed houses, and camels, and donkeys, and picturesque water sellers in bright red fezzes and yellow jackets, looked in the glare of the noon-day sun like one of the cities of the east that we had read about as youngsters in the "Arabian Nights." Our time was now getting short so we said good-bye to the cheery corporal and forming our party up we got back to the barracks as quickly as possible, where after a farewell dinner with our kind hosts, we packed our belongings (mostly dirty linen) and just managed to catch our train back to Alexandria.*

Cairo must be one of the most polluted cities on the planet. Smog from industry and the huge number of cars on the streets mean that people wake up (as I did) to a thick haze each morning. Sometimes this burns off by midday; more often it simply gets worse unless there is a breeze. As grandfather says, the citadel is situated on the highest point of Cairo; as we approached, the Mosque of Mohammed Ali Pasha rose out of the smog blanket like a silvery space ship, its huge dome surmounting the fortifications. These were constructed not by Mohammed Ali Pasha but by Saladin in 1183 to protect the government complex and palaces from the

Crusaders. It remained the seat of government until the 1860's. The huge mosque which bears his name was built by Mohammed Ali Pasha in 1857 as a snub to the former Turkish rulers. Although Turkish himself he is regarded as the founder of modern Egypt, laying the foundations of an industrial and commercial era. The mosque was designed by a Turkish architect and, to add further insult to injury, its form followed that prescribed by the Sultan of Turkey who had not decreed its construction. Rumour has it that the architect was put to the sword for his deception. Our guide was a delightful, well-informed young woman, a history student paying her way through university. She offered Jay and me her services as we were standing at the entrance to the mosque. She had a wide open face with a friendly smile. She was dressed in a cream coloured tunic with a headscarf and spoke perfect English. Just like grandfather we donned blue standard-issue slippers although not over our shoes, which we had to leave on a shelf outside the main doorway. There was enough light from the large chandeliers and the wide ring of hanging lamps for me to be overwhelmed by the intricate designs and the cavernous dome stretching above. Our guide told us that the central dome is 21 meters in diameter and 52 meters high. The colours are predominantly gold and ochre with columns and walls of alabaster; hence its nickname: "Alabaster Mosque." Four smaller domes and four semicircular ones surround the main one. Lying back on the red carpet is the best way to take it all in. The lights create pinpoints like stars in the lofty vault of heaven. The lower gallery round the central dome has a series of little windows in bright red, blue and yellow colours. The dome itself is decorated with inlaid geometrical shapes in segments leading one's eye to a central motif like a mandala. The predominant colours are green and gold while the small domes are decorated in dark green and silver designs. The semi-circular ones are dark blue and gold and there are ornate

Arabic calligraphy designs at the top of each supporting arch. Grandfather refers to the ornate carpet on which worshippers squat or kneel; the carpet is still there but it has been sliced up into smaller sections for ease of maintenance, the guide told us. Sad. She pointed out Mohammed Ali's ornate tomb and the set of stone stairs leading up to a covered landing – the minbar. The Imam gives his Friday address one step down from the top landing which is reserved for the prophet himself.

Outside is a large courtyard with a fountain in the centre for ritual washing before prayers. On one side is an ornamental clock in a lacy tower presented to Mohammed Ali by Louis Philippe, King of France. The mechanism was damaged in transit and has never worked but the king had no such mechanical difficulty with the magnificent obelisk from Luxor he received in return. It stands in the Place de la Concorde in Paris. The view across Cairo to the pyramids at Giza would have been magnificent were it not for the hazy smog. The guide took us to the Bijou Palace alongside the mosque and we saw three reception rooms where Mohammed Ali received officials and dignitaries. The palace housed his offices. Only three of the three hundred rooms are open to the public; I thought the baths with the eunuch's spy hole described in the preceding section by grandfather were somewhere in this complex but not open to view. Later I found the baths in what is now a military museum dedicated to the exploits of modern and ancient Egypt. This complex was once three palaces known as the Harem Palaces and is decorated lavishly in the baroque style with floral decorations, columns and fountains painted on side panels, staircases and corridors. The ceilings are lavishly decorated in raised geometric shapes. The walls and floors of the baths are white marble and the decorated ceilings are supported by slender marble columns. Underneath the stained-glass windows are battle scenes and portraits of military leaders; an incongruous contrast to the view of naked ladies my grandfather and the British sergeant imagined through the eunuch's peephole. Satin ropes prevented me from getting close enough to find the peephole itself.

Outside amidst the display of tanks, guns and fighter aircraft stands a statue of Mohammed Ali's son, Ibraham Pasha seated on a horse with his right hand raised pointing into the middle distance.

Islam is integrated into daily life – it's a mosque a minute as your taxi whizzes you around Cairo. Five times a day the call to prayer broadcasts out all over the city. In the local cafes there is a space set aside for prayer with rugs provided at no charge. The sailors who manned the felucca we sailed on overnight from Luxor would take turns kneeling for prayer. In 2009 there was a terrible train crash outside Cairo. The engine of the first train was disabled in a collision with a cow. The driver got no answer to his emergency call because the operator at headquarters had left his post briefly to pray and a second train crashed into the stationary one with considerable loss of life. I imagine that Egyptian Railways will employ prayer substitutes to cover such incidents in future. However I realized that technology trumps religion when I saw a woman in full burka with a slit for only one eye using a cell phone.

## ALEXANDRIA

The train to Alexandria runs through rich agricultural land on either side of the Nile. 96% of Egyptians live on this strip which is only 4% of the total area of the country. Rainfall in Egypt is negligible except on the coast where Alexandria is situated. Most of the farms seemed to be smallholdings worked by families. I saw men, women and children harvesting vegetables or working in large fields of grain. I would guess from what I saw that there is little mechanization. I did see a number of ox plows with a driver walking behind but very few tractors. Grandfather describes seeing primitive water wheels or scoops. I presume these have been replaced by pumps and generators for I did not see any. Irrigation canals are everywhere.

*A wireless message was received ordering us back to Malta, owing to an outbreak of war between Italy and Turkey. The air was full of buzzes and rumors and wars and echoes of wars. We had come round under easy steam but as soon as our Captain returned from the flagship we knew something was in the wind. Steam was ordered for 18 knots and we were off to some unknown destination, steaming east under sealed orders. We learned in due course that Alexandria was our destination and I nearly wept when I thought about my washing lying snugly in the washerwoman's' house in Valetta and me without a white suit or a change of linen. We arrived at Alexandria on Saturday forenoon where everything was calm and peaceful and tied up in a leisurely manner, head and stern, opposite the Khedive's Palace.*

*Leave was granted as usual and I went ashore and had a look round the city. They say that all roads lead to Rome but in Alexandria all roads lead to the Grand Square, where all the business houses and the best cafes are situated. A fine bronze statue of Mohamed Ali Pasha on horseback occupies the central position in the square. The cafes here extend right into the street and are used mostly by the better class Egyptians, who look very picturesque in their smart cut European clothes and bright red fezzes.*

For grandfather all roads led to the Grand Square; not so in my case. I hailed a taxi from the Sheraton hotel situated in the suburb of Montazah some forty minutes from the centre. Taxi drivers refer to this beachfront area as "Miami." A funny thing happened on the way to the forum: I told the taxi driver I wanted to go to the central square; he said "Downtown?" and I agreed. After driving along on a freeway a while I realized we had turned away from the centre. Before I could question him the driver pulled up in front of a motel named "The Downtown." It took an hour in congested traffic to retrace our way to the Grand Square. The square is still grand and most of the buildings grandfather describes still stand with the elegant Cecil Hotel (now Sofitel) a centerpiece. The bronze statue of the Pasha still looks out to sea but he is no longer on horseback. I had seen the original displayed outside the National Military Museum in Cairo.

*Leaving the brilliantly lighted square, a few steps bring one straight into Arab slumdom. The houses are mere hovels and the smells emanating from them suggest anything from romance to enteric. The inhabitants seem to take life in true eastern fashion and spend the most of their time squatting outside their miserable dwellings.*

Changes have been made over the last one hundred years; the rabbit warren of poor hovels behind the square has been replaced by tall tenements with opulent little fashion boutiques and shoe shops on street level and vertical housing above. I assume that the poor have been moved further from the centre as the rents for such high rise living would be beyond their means.

*The Arabs are a queer people but we must remember that they are old in civilization and have forgotten more than we have learned. They are fanatics as regards their religion and during our stay we had many evidences of their blind devotion to Mohammed. The Arabs in Tripoli, and many from Egypt, were assisting the Turks to repel the Italians who had descended on their coasts like highway robbers, - and let one say what one likes it developed into a Holy war - the cross against the crescent. The torch, once lit in Tripoli was a signal to arms right through Egypt and many Arabs flocked to join the Turks, and everyone embracing the Christian faith was looked upon as an enemy. During the "Feast of the Holy Carpet" ( a quaint Mohammedan religious ceremony), the Arabs worked themselves into such a state of religious frenzy that the Europeans deemed it the best policy to stay indoors and all leave for soldiers and sailors was stopped. Landing parties of both services, with ball cartridge, were kept in readiness for the purpose of maintaining order by force if the occasion arose. Nothing of a serious nature took place while we lay there but every Italian reverse was the signal for demonstrations against the Italian residents and some severe street fighting took place, revolvers and cudgels being freely used.*

*While lying at Alexandria our ships' company had the good fortune to witness one of nature's phenomena in the shape of a twin waterspout. It appeared to be about 3 miles outside the breakwater and stretched from the sea like two huge pillars right up to the clouds. The land batteries fired several shots at it but whether they hit it or whether it had run its course I cannot tell but at all events it broke just outside the harbour, one end flying upwards and the other falling into the sea, causing an upheaval like a gigantic submarine explosion.*

I knew about two features of ancient Alexandria: the lighthouse on the island of Pharos at the entrance to the harbour and the library. The lighthouse, which was one of the seven wonders of the ancient world, has long since gone although Fort Qaitbey on the point of the Eastern breakwater contains some of its pink granite stones. The vast library was burned by the Roman forces under Julius Caesar, although historians dispute the accounts. UNESCO funded the building of a new library which opened in 2002. It is utterly magnificent. It is shaped like a discus lying at an angle towards the north so that the windows do not allow the sun's harmful rays to penetrate the interior. Looking up at its open seven storey interior from the foyer brought tears to my eyes. It is spacious and lined with light-coloured wood. Books are housed on low, free standing sets of shelves preserving the open feel to each floor.

On my second day in Alexandria I walked along El Corniche, the gorgeous, curving seafront roadway lined with scads of hotels and older apartment buildings. I fell into step with a man ahead of me. We began talking as we walked. Hassan was a journalist and a poet who had lived most of his life in Alexandria. He was a man of medium height, solidly built, and neatly dressed in jeans with a well-worn brown leather jacket, striped shirt and a distinctive green corduroy cap. His wide face was nut-brown with engaging dark eyes, pronounced laugh lines and a ready smile. He had a habit of cocking his head to one side when listening to you; paying close attention without interrupting or taking over the conversation. I would describe him as alert and sensitive. He told me that he had lived in France and then in Russia, where he met a girl who had broken his heart.

He asked why I was visiting Alexandria so I told him about following in the tracks of my grandfather. He asked what I had not yet seen and offered to show me the naval harbour where grandfather would have landed. He haggled with the taxi driver before we set off. We were not allowed inside the ornate gateway so we peered through it at the docks with cranes busily unloading ships. Next to the gateway was a long driveway lined with shrubs with beautifully manicured green lawns on each side. Hassan told me that the huge white building barely visible from the locked gateway had been one of King Farouk's palaces and, before that, the Khedive's palace alongside which HMS Lancaster had been berthed. He then suggested showing me 'his' Alexandria so we started at the oldest coffee house in the city – a large, rather dusty establishment with wooden tables and a prayer space in one corner facing Mecca. Prayer mats are provided for the clientele taking a break from their hookahs and their drinks. The place was crowded mainly with men playing dominoes and drinking tea from glass cups with mint leaves on the side or tiny cups of sweet black coffee served in a briki. After coffee he recited some of his poems about love and nature written in both English and Arabic. They were beautifully poignant. We then went by taxi through narrow back streets to the Souk where we saw carved wooden furniture – chairs, sofas and armoires - being made. The market had specialized areas; furniture in one, scarves and clothing in another and carvings in yet another. Sales and manufacturing were side by side.

We were hungry after all our sightseeing so Hassan asked if I liked fish. "Definitely," said I so we walked to the fish market where we selected those we fancied from the icy slabs of fresh fish. They were cooked in the open kitchen while we were served plates of salad and fresh crusty bread.

Yum! And more yums when the shrimps and fillets arrived. As the meal was cleared away by the super-efficient wait team I wondered whether grandfather ate fish or whether he had as much antipathy for seafood as he did for the ocean. After the meal and coffee in another coffee house we said our sad farewells and hugged one another. I went back to my hotel, marveling at how instant a connection with a stranger can be.

That evening I mused about grandfather's description of the enmity between the "Cross and the Crescent" displayed in the conflict between Italy and Turkey. Hassan and I had related like long lost friends, not even conscious of our Muslim and Christian backgrounds. Yet the old enmity between nations has not changed a great deal over the past hundred years, as shown by the bitter anti-Arab feelings in the US since the bombings of 9/11 and the policies of Canada and most Western countries over the Palestinian issue.

## PORT SAID

Grandfather and I shared the same final destination in Egypt - Port Said – which Jay and I reached on a rattly three-hour bus ride through dusty town after dusty industrial town. The Cairo bus station was underneath an ultra-modern multi-level shopping mall with indoor parking and chrome in plenty. The Port Said terminal was squalid by comparison, situated in the port area close to main street shops dating from the late 1800's. The first I saw was a colonial-looking Woolworths with a wrapround verandah and a balcony above. This two storey style was common; some of the upper level balconies had lacy metal railings and overhangs like those in the French quarter of New Orleans. The streets were laid out in a grid pattern and were filled with people. After a snack lunch we headed for the canal area where large ships were anchored at the entrance before making their way slowly through the town.

*The Suez Canal is a great sight, and ships of all countries pass daily on their way to or from the Orient. There is a statue of de Lesseps at the entrance and the sculptor has portrayed him with his hand pointing to the opening of this wonderful waterway to the east. Rudyard Kipling in his poem "On the road to Mandalay" makes his soldier say:*

*"Ship me somewheres east of Suez, where the best is like the worst,*
*Where there aren't no Ten Commandments an' a man can raise a thirst."*

*Good old Kipling! He says he can hear the east a' calling him. Well I hope it never calls on me. If it does I shall pack, pack as far west as I can get. Scotland with its fogs and rain, its frosts and snows is good enough for me.*

*The canteen in Port Said was at one time a huge hotel, built by a Dutch firm for the purpose of putting up travellers from the ships arriving too late for going through the canal. With the advent of the electric light it became possible for ships to go through during the hours of darkness and in consequence the trade of the hotel was ruined and our benevolent admiralty took it over and made it into a canteen and stationed a ship at Port Said to support this admirable institution.*

The "huge hotel" with grandfather's canteen has been replaced by two modern hotels in a ghastly pseudo Art Deco style and a building with fake Gothic towers housing the

96

Egyptian Shooting Club. And all that is left of the imposing statue of de Lesseps is the enormous twenty five foot high plinth. I discovered that the statue was removed in 1956 when President Nasser nationalized the canal and gave Britain and the allies the monumental finger. It has been refurbished with funds from France but has not been resurrected. Apparently it stands forsaken *sans* plinth in a tiny garden inside a shipyard in Port Fouad west of the canal. I did see a series of bronze plaques along the adjoining walkway depicting the construction of the canal. The final one shows Nasser in a similar pose to de Lesseps with his hand gesturing towards the East over the Port Authority building and the canal.

*There are many Parsee fortune tellers here with wonderful credentials, suave manners and smooth tongues. They do their business mostly among callers from passing ships and one can get a good past and a rosy future for the outlay of a sixpence. The street vendors are the most persistent I have ever met, but then they have to catch their customers either hurrying from a ship on returning to one and therefore have to hustle. We seemed to be settled here for some time and to vary the theme I propose to deal with a subject that I have long since had in my mind. I should imagine that Egypt in general and Port Said in particular is a paradise for the pedlar, but the reverse to anyone else in a country where the thermometer is not exerting itself at all at 120 degrees - and where none of the plagues - darkness, boils, flies or bites - were ever really stayed, in spite of all assurances to the contrary. A good working plan when dealing with native pedlars is to believe half what they say (you can choose which half) and to pay them a quarter of what they ask. Reduce their shillings to piastres, and divide by four; then, when you have generously conceded a small advance on that, you will probably have given twice what the thing is worth.*

*I shall never forget my railway ride to Cairo. When I got out to get a cup of coffee at Tanrah I had to fight the flies for it. But that you can do any day in Egypt, where everything that isn't mosquitoes is flies. The hawkers you have always with you. Half a dozen of them would set you up in decent housekeeping in an hour and, what an Egyptian can't hawk, no one else will find it worth their while to try and sell. The water man comes first with his cry of "Moya". He gives you a small supply of the precious fluid, unfiltered probably, and certainly germinous, from a "goolah" - the quaint native water cooler, shaped like an urn, and with perforations across the top, about five inches from the mouth, to keep the dust out. Any Egyptian would be lost without his "goolah", and they must be made by the million. Kench is the place they come from and only Kench mud will make them - porous and yet watertight. The constant slow evaporation which takes place makes "goolah" water always fairly cool. The travelling native drinks from his goolah, washes from it, cleanses his fruit in the charitable mouth - does everything in fact but bath in it; and that probably only because bathing is not a favorite exercise with him. When an Arab moves he takes a goolah apiece for each of his wives, an angerib for himself to sleep in, a deck-chair for himself to sit on, a coffee-pot to make his coffee in, and a stone to grind it with; and his household goods are complete. All those things go on baggage-camels, travelling at the rate of two miles an hour, across the great desert; and on any odd corners of his camel van which are not occupied he hangs more goolahs.*

*The bread-man runs the water man very close as a peripatetic pedlar; carrying his wares through the streets with a cry of "Aish- Aish". An Arab baker is rather suggestive of a soiled snowflake. He carries the native bread in rings either on his arms or piled up on a tray slung from his shoulders. With his goolah full of water, and his rings of bread, the travelling Arab can dine well and if the bread-man cries "Aish wa bud taxal" he can have a feast indeed for he knows that the bread man carries fresh eggs as well as bread. They are Egyptian eggs, fresh indeed, but so small that they would be disowned by any self-respecting pigeon in England. A very good light repast can be had anywhere in Egypt at a small cost if one knows what to buy. Green figs, seven for a penny, and a water-melon or three pomegranates for your other half-piastre (1 1/4d) make up a meal such as Omar Khayyam might have envied you.*

*Most travelling Arabs carry their baggage, picturesquely, in vivid squares of cotton, tied together as the British workman ties his dinner, by the four corners. Nearly every type and nationality can be seen in Port Said in colors ranging from white to jet black. We were greatly taken up with the wonderful costumes and glaring colors. The Egyptian man typically dresses in a long loose skirt, an English cover coat and a red fez with a black tassel, something like a smoking cap at home. The women are as gorgeously apparelled as any Solomon in black satiny gowns sparkling with sequins, with multitudinous petticoats (which they take care to show), and high-heeled shoes of white satin to which a generous quantity of Egyptian mud generally adheres. Their arms, necks and ears are usually loaded with jewellery; but the rest of their wardrobe- probably their at home gowns, - are contained in the bundles referred to.*

There has been a distinct change in everyday dress from grandfather's time. Most women, particularly younger ones, dress in a head scarf (or hijab) with a blouse and either pants or jeans underneath a short skirt. Some wear long gowns but I saw only a few in full black burkas with eye slits. Men have largely opted for conventional Western clothes although I did see a few in long robes. The red fez with a black tassel is definitely out; the only place I saw them was at a curio stall at the Citadel in Cairo.

*Ancient pottery most people buy in Cairo; but it just as cheap and genuine at any of the stations en route, and you have this advantage - that your dealer must clinch his bargain quietly or the train moves on, leaving you with the goods, and the dealer "mafish fulus" - without the money. But the staple industry of Egypt is the manufacture of antiques. A dab of Nile mud, roughly fashioned in the shape of some insect unknown to entomoligists, but confidently asserted to be a Scarab is colored not too highly, and buried, perhaps one minute for each of its reputed years. There you have an antique lamp of which the number made might well have lighted to paradise every soul that has ever died in Egypt - unbeliever or faithful.*

*We had almost begun to look forward to spending Xmas in Port Said when a message was received on board which sent us hurrying away from Dutch House in as dramatic a manner as we had tied up to it. We were to join our squadron once more and the first stage of our journey was Malta where we arrived on the afternoon of Tuesday the 19th.*

After a fruitless search for WW1 naval artifacts in the local war museum and a walk along the beach we decided to return to Cairo on the evening bus. Sunday traffic meant that the driver took detours through crowded little towns, sometimes on one way streets, to avoid the congestion on the major highway. The three hour return trip took five hours which seemed even longer because our ears were not tuned to loud Arabic music. The following day I took leave of Egypt and of Jay and flew to Corfu where it was cold and teeming with rain.

# CHAPTER 6: GREECE

## CORFU

By morning the teeming showers of my evening arrival in Corfu had given way to sullen grey clouds. The hotel manager gave me directions to the centre of town which, he said, was about an hour's walk away along the sea front. I took my umbrella and wore a warm jacket to ward off the cold January wind. The houses in the suburb in which the Hotel Bretagne was situated looked to be about 1920's vintage with red tiled roofs and pastel-shaded walls. Corfu is known as the green island in contrast to the arid, rocky Cyclades south of Athens – Mykonos, Paros, Naxos. The trees on the way were a mix of large twisty olives, pointed pencil pines, wide bay trees and a multitude of palms. After a brisk ten minutes I arrived at a wide pavement of irregular stones, flanking the sea wall along the edge of the coastline. Occasionally there was a spattering of rain. The iron lamp posts at regular intervals were intricately carved and the lamps themselves were shaped like old fashioned gas lanterns. Low hazy blue hills looked out to the sea, melding into the grey water at the horizon; gradually the sky began to clear and patches of blue appeared, revealing the distant mountains of Albania capped with snow and sunlight.

As I walked further along, the suburban houses gave way to older Italianate style houses and grand-looking hotels. The pavement turned away from the water at the lower bastions of the citadel and I climbed up to the old city with the fortifications on my right and a large green square (one of the largest in Europe as I later found out) on my left.

*The town of Corfu is not very interesting in itself but the surroundings are beautiful and the varied panorama of mountain, orange groves and calm peaceful islands dotted over the blue waters of the Mediterranean forms a picture that impresses even the experienced tourist and puts the true lover of nature in ecstasies.*

Clearly grandfather was a lover of nature and not of cities because, unlike him, I was stunned by the beauty of Corfu town, which is on the east coast of the island. Two massive fortresses dominate the approach to the harbour from the sea. Between them lies what I would describe as an ornate version of Venice but, in place of canals, there are twisted and narrow medieval lanes adjoining wide boulevards. On a green sward in the centre there is a legacy of the British protectorate—which lasted from 1814 to 1863 – a cricket field directly in front of the palace of St Michael and St George built for the British governor in 1819. I discovered that the island boasts no less than five cricket teams who do battle on that pitch. Did grandfather play? His twin sons were devotees of the game; I recalled watching them play for their respective village clubs in Scotland in 1948. Jim was out for a duck but Colin took three wickets with his medium pace bowling. From the Venetian occupation (1401 to 1797) the Corfuits inherited a magnificent colonnade with an arcade of shops modelled on the Rue de Rivoli in Paris and, from the English occupation, a Regency style palace overlooking a cricket field. Oh the joys of Empire!

Adjoining the cricket field is a spacious park with an ornate wrought-iron bandstand or pavilion, where the local

Philharmonic orchestra gives concerts, a fountain, and a circular monument commemorating the second governor, Sir Thomas Maitland. Separating the park and the field is the inevitable car park. Corfu is overrun with vehicles. I sat in the park absorbing the weak winter sun and thought about the differences in Corfu, Cairo and other cities on grandfather's itinerary between one hundred years ago and today. Traffic now crowds streets which were not designed for it, huge car parks dominate historic centres like the one in front of me. Motorways slice over old neighbourhoods. Pedestrians are consigned to secondary roles. How different it would all seem were grandfather to see it now. The smog in Cairo which prevents a clear view of the pyramids from the city would not have been there in his time. Then there is the universal problem of disposal. Acres of city land given over to dumps. And in North America the proliferation of drive-in fast food outlets, banks and supermarkets means we are increasingly dependent on vehicle traffic for our everyday needs. Progress has come at an incredible price, I thought.

Gazing out to sea near the park is a statue of Ioannis Kapodistrias, a local hero who became the first president of the newly independent Greece in 1828. I crossed the park and made my way down the old streets to the bustling centre where I stopped for lunch at a family-run restaurant serving local dishes such as pastitsada (pasta with veal), bourdetto (cod in pepper sauce), and rabbit stew, which I ate. Sitting opposite me in the crowded restaurant was a dark-haired, middle-aged man who looked like Al Pacino. He was flattered when I walked over and told him so; he had no compunction about allowing me to take his photograph for the Canadians back home.

The Austro-Hungarian Empire of Franz Josef and his consort, Elizabeth (known as Sissy), was a focus for me the following day when I visited the Achilleion, Sissy's palace 10 kilometers south of Corfu. I have long admired her for her rebellion against the shackles of court life and her spirited search for Greek culture. She has been dubbed the "Tragic Empress" for losing her beloved son, Rudolph, to suicide and her own life to a random assassination by an anarchist. Grandfather visited the palace in 1911 after the German Kaiser, Wilhelm, purchased it in 1907:

*The Emperor of Germany has a palace here and, as may be supposed, it contains many gems of the painter's and sculptor's art. On the broad terrace approaching from the roadway are the famous statues of the Greek wrestlers. Executed in bronze and perfectly nude they stand on pedestals on either side of the terrace in the ready position for a bout and seem to the onlooker to have been suddenly arrested by the touch of a fairy's wand and are only awaiting the spell to be broken so that they might come to grips. Another statue well worthy of mentioning is a bronze cast of Achilles by a German Professor. Who has not heard the legend of Achilles? How he was dipped in the water by his mother to make him invulnerable against offensive weapons. How she forgot to dip the part she hung on to, namely his heel and how his enemy found the secret out and aimed an arrow at the vulnerable part and caused his death. This statue is a copy from the original, and is a marvel of the sculptor's art. The professor has caught the expression perfectly of a man dying in agony, and probably what to Achilles was more humiliating; the fact that his enemy had found out his secret and brought low this hero of so many triumphs.*

*On the front of the residence are full sized marble statues representing the death of Achilles - a well known masterpiece. I have never seen anything as finely chiselled as this exquisite work of art. A bronze cast of the same hero by a German Professor is rather an imposing figure, standing some thirty feet high, but it lacks the fine proportion and natural expression of the sculptor's delicate work on the marble statues. On a terrace at the back of the Palace are statues in marble representing the nine muses and the guide had a long story to tell about the history of each, to repeat which, I am afraid, would weary my reader.*

The courtyard of the nine muses, which adjoins the palace, has a checkered black and white tiled floor with a pool in the centre. Overlooking the pool is a marble statue of Dionysus as a young boy on the shoulders of a Satyr. They gaze fondly into one another's eyes. I was reminded of my father's last visit to my home in Guelph. After a walk along the river we came back to my driveway where I suggested that we re-enact the flight of Aeneas and his father, Anchises, from the burning city of Troy. As in that account by Virgil, I invited my father to climb onto my back so that I could carry him to the back door. He questioned whether his weight would be too much for me; I assured him he would not. At 86 he had shrunk considerably from his once six foot frame. By the time we reached the back door we were in tears; both deeply touched by the experience. He had been a Classics Professor and I had studied the story in a Latin class with him. I gazed down at my reflection in the pool lined with water lilies. I wondered whether grandfather had stared down at his reflection; if so, was his image preserved beneath mine in the dark water?

106

*There is a striking picture over the grand staircase depicting Achilles in a happier scene than that portrayed in the statue of marble. It is called "The Triumph of Achilles" and shows him in his chariot entering the city of Troy dragging Hector and, I think, Agamemnon at the chariot wheels. The people are seen on the walls and house tops cheering frantically and the whole forms a most impressive picture. The overhead pictures in the dining and smoking rooms are splendid works of art and beyond the power of my poor pen to describe.*

After various incarnations, including a recent stint as a casino, the Palace is now owned by the Greek government. They have restored the exterior and furnished the interior with many of Sissy's belongings: furniture, artwork and curios. It is now a museum. I discovered that the James Bond film, "For Your Eyes Only", was shot there during the time it was a casino. The grounds are filled with sculptures she collected or commissioned. Achilles was her hero and there is a moving piece by the German Professor, Ernst Gustav Herter, showing Achilles' death agonies as he tries to pull Paris's fatal arrow from his heel. Apparently Kaiser Bill did not approve of the hero's death adorning the front of his palace so he had it moved to the back and replaced with the vulgar statue of Achilles, the Conqueror, triumphantly standing over 30 feet high at the entrance. The Kaiser commissioned this work from the Berlin sculptor, Johannes Gotz in 1910.

The spectacularly white palace dominates the hill on which it stands. The facade has every known style of Greek column and adornment. While it does have the look of an ornate wedding cake, I would not go so far as Henry Miller who described it as "the worst piece of gimcrackery I'd ever laid eyes on" and thought it "would make an excellent museum for surrealistic art". I found the artwork grandfather describes including the huge oil painting over a staircase showing the body of Hector (not Agamemnon) being dragged round the walls of Troy but not into the city itself as Grandfather thought. The Trojans are not cheering from the walls either; together with their King, Priam, they are mourning the death of Hector. It is a pity that grandfather's guide did not mention Sissy, for he would surely have approved of her rebellion against the stuffiness of her husband (Emperor Franz Josef) and his court. She took every opportunity to escape from Vienna and sail around her beloved Mediterranean in her yacht. She was keen to learn all she could in her travels: she visited the site of the newly excavated city of Troy and became acquainted with its discoverer, the archaeologist Heinrich Schliemann. She learned Greek and enjoyed meeting with ordinary people in different parts of the country. It is said that on one state occasion she had her hairdresser don her finery to impersonate her while she was rowed ashore in plain clothes to mingle with people at a local market.

Grandfather's socialist sympathies would probably have sided with the group in Corfu who, in 1911, organized the first trade union in Greece which went on strike that same year to demand the reinstatement of three men at a local factory and a reduction of the workday from 14 hours to 12. They were successful. I imagine he would also have been moved by the memorial on the main street to Kostas Georgakis - a young student who sacrificed his life in 1970 by setting himself on fire for the sake of freedom and democracy in Greece, which was then a military dictatorship..

*There are many evidences in and around Corfu that Lord Byron is immortalized in the hearts of the Greek people. Besides a statue in bronze there are many of his sayings and extracts from his poems displayed on the walls of the houses in and around Corfu.*

A marble statue of him still stands in the lush garden below the palace terrace. Byron, his hair neat and curly, is seated on an armchair, his long cloak draped and folded over the chair, reaching down to a buckled shoe with a modest high heel. His expression is thoughtful, his eyebrows somewhat puzzled. His jaw leans on the thumb and fingers of his left hand; his left elbow draped over the edge of his armrest. His right hand presses a notebook into his left knee. His posture is languorous, and at odds with the searching expression in his face.

I walked back to the bus stop along the ridge, looking down to the sea far below. I saw an island with a tiny, whitewashed church joined to the mainland by a causeway. I made my way down the steep hillside by a convenient stairway and crossed the causeway to the island. The church was linked to a monastery; I later discovered from my guidebook that the view from the hillside is featured in many postcards and in travel brochures. I was startled by the roar of an airliner flying low overhead; I realized that this idyllic island lies on the final flight path to Corfu International Airport nearby. I was struck by the contrast between the centuries.

109

*Turning to another side of the picture one cannot avoid, even among those evidences of the prowess and valour of the freedom loving Greeks, seeing signs of ruin and decay in the nation as a whole. I am afraid the women of Greece are not honoured as they used to be if we can believe our history. I saw many of them working in the fields, swinging a heavy implement like a great hoe, turning over the soil and standing in slush and mud up to their ankles and whether from necessity or preference utterly destitute of shoes or stockings. Another lot were carrying baskets of stones on their heads to mend the roads and yet another lot carrying faggots of wood to burn for charcoal. These are living statues that can be seen and the wretched appearance of these human beasts of burden appealed more to me than all the bronze and marble that ever was dug from the earth. I think when a nation forgets to honor the maid and the mother and drives them to earn a subsistence wage in the factory or the field then that nation is failing in its duty to the children and must, like Greece, develop eventually into a has-been. I am afraid that anyone who knows their Greece from the pages of romantic story would be sadly disappointed in the Greece of today and I sincerely wish they may never be disillusioned but that they may hug the Greece they know in their bosoms and cherish it there.*

That night in my draughty bedroom I considered the views my grandfather expressed about the decline of Greece reflected by women he saw doing manual labour in the fields and on the highways. It would be easy to dismiss his views as being simply the product of his times, especially his conviction that a woman's place is in the home with her children rather than being part of the work force. It is true that

110

women have undergone a huge emancipation since his time. However what I have observed in Greece is that men have not altered in the same way those in Britain and North America have. There appears to be a strong cultural bias that defines the male role as breadwinner and master. Pubs and cafes are the domains of men and one seldom sees fathers pushing buggies or playing with young children in parks or playgrounds as one does in the West. Housework and child rearing are more closely circumscribed as woman's work in Greece. So I do have some sympathy for grandfather's views that Greek culture has not kept pace with the times.

## CHIOS

*We left this isolated village (*Marmaris in Turkey*) on Saturday the 15th for Kios, an island in the Grecian Archipelago, and arrived at the town of Schios on the Sunday afternoon. The town looked very clean and new, no doubt owing to the fact that it was visited by an earthquake some twenty years ago, which destroyed most of the old houses. On the slopes of the hills are many beautiful gardens and nearly every kind of fruit can be grown to perfection here. The principal fruits grown are apples, pears, plums, oranges, lemons, almonds, pomegranates, olives and quinces. The gardens are watered by means of irrigation and the water which is drawn from depths varying from 30 to 50 feet is as clear as crystal and cold as ice. How nice it was for us to stand by the wheels and catch the water in an old Greek jar and drink it and love our lands in it. It was the best and coldest water we had tasted since leaving England.*

*The people were exceptionally hospitable and how kindly they treated us. We were honoured guests wherever we went and they brought for our consumption the finest liqueurs and sweetmeats. One sweetmeat we enjoyed very much we found to be the flower of the lemon tree. How we rolled it on our tongues and smacked our lips and washed it down with ice cold water and cracked jokes with the kindly people. What simple homely lives, what healthy and numerous children, what stalwart sons and comely daughters. If ever I could afford a holiday in the Mediterranean I should spend it among the Greek fruit-growers on the slopes of the mountains above Schios.*

From Corfu in the west I flew to Chios, an island on the eastern side of mainland Greece. It lies just west of Turkey; in fact I could see the Turkish coast from my cold, draughty room overlooking the harbour. The atmosphere, the view and the price ($37 per night) made up for the discomfort. Besides, there were fleecy rugs stowed away in the closet and I needed them night and day. Like grandfather, I loved Chios. The people I met on my trips round the town and in the countryside were friendly and helpful. They were pleased to be asked questions about their lives and their customs; many spoke good English and some had lived abroad. I bought a jar of lemon flower preserve and it certainly lived up to the lip-smacking qualities he describes. As did the cool, clear water from the underground wells he enjoyed. However, it is no longer drawn up in buckets.

Grandfather's comment about choosing to spend a holiday in Chios if he could afford it underlined a contrast in our lives. I have always been able to travel to other countries, even as a student in England spending a Christmas break in Spain or as a young psychologist holidaying in the Caribbean. My career choices too were much more open than his; I started

112

in industry, lectured at universities in three different countries and finally became a psychologist in private practice.

I discovered other things about Chios. In grandfather's time it was ruled by the Turks but eighteen months after he was there the Greeks defeated the Turkish fleet in a naval battle just off Chios and regained control of the island. It has a rich seafaring history and a third of all Greek ship owners are from Chios. I was surprised when asked the inevitable first question: "Where you from?" how many had been to Canada. And the inevitable answer to my question about how they knew Canada was: "I was seaman on ship." Chiots claim that Homer was born on the island; however so do Greeks from seven other places. Another legend has Homer declaiming his tales to groups of citizens and apprentice story-tellers on a rock not far from the town. The rock (known as Daskalopetra or teacher's rock) is on a commanding ledge above the sea and forms a natural pulpit from which one can imagine the exploits of Odysseus ringing out. I believe grandfather would have enjoyed that Homeric myth. Given his sweet tooth (the lemon drops) he might also have enjoyed the local cookies made from mastic, a resin produced by a low shrub unique to the island. The locals enjoy it in many forms: a natural chewing gum, toothpaste, hand cream, shampoo and a full range of spa products. Mastic is reputed to have medical benefits such as lowering cholesterol levels and preventing tooth decay. I can imagine grandfather being skeptical of those claims.

The town shows little sign of the destruction wrought by the earthquake grandfather describes although few early buildings survive, except in two outlying villages: the medieval, fortress-like town of Mesta and the painted town of Pyrgi, Mesta's stone dwellings and stores are all linked by

113

narrow laneways, maze-like, between them. The buildings in Pyrgi are decorated with intricate grey and white geometrical shapes. I was told that each house carries a coded message for future generations of the family and that the patterns are laboriously scratched or etched on the walls. First the stonework is covered with a plaster layer mixed with grey sand then coated with whitewash. The white is then scratched off to produce the final design. One design I saw implores children of the family who have emigrated to return on their grandparents' anniversary. When a friend explained this meaning, it struck a chord because my travels with grandfather and his diary have brought me closer to him.

## CHANIA

*Alas! Our dreams of ivy and wall flowers in Malta were destined to be rudely shattered. A signal was received at three o'clock on Sunday morning the 25th ordering us to coal and provision ship at dawn and be ready to proceed to sea as soon as possible. The coal arrived about six o'clock and an early start was made to lump it in-board. Some trouble in Crete was the cause of the bustle and commotion, and about two o'clock in the afternoon, having coaled and provisioned ship, we steamed out of the Grand Harbour and proceeded eastwards. We arrived off Chania, the capital town of the island, on Tuesday morning and dropped anchor in the bay. The town looked rather pretty from the ship, but the cause of many bloody massacres could be easily seen in the shape of several mosques with their tall, tapering minarets (dwarfed by the towering snow-covered mountains in the background) projecting skywards from the flat-roofed houses like giant spears. I do not meant to infer that the Mohammedan religion is more aggressive or bloodthirsty than any other brand but it does not seem to blend harmoniously with the Christian kind*

114

*on this island. Ever since I could read a newspaper there have been frequent leading articles headed "Trouble in the Near East". Christians murdering Jews and Turks murdering Christians and all for the glory of God.*

*"Is it not a mad world my masters?"*

I encountered a problem with my pronunciation of Greek when I hailed a taxi after landing at the airport in Chania. I asked the driver to take me to Ifigenia Rooms, the lodgings I had booked on the internet. He did not understand my request until I handed him a written copy of the reservation. "Ah, Ifichenya," he said, with a guttural "g." and an accent on the 'en.' I had pronounced it as I had been taught to say it in Classical Culture lectures on Euripides play "Iphigenia in Aulis." - "eye-phi-jen-eye-a"- with the accent on the "eye." Accenting the correct syllable is crucial in Greek, as I was to discover on the road to Delphi. When I asked the way to Delphi people would stare at me blankly until I learned to pronounce it Delphi. The cab driver spoke surprisingly good English and negotiated his way through the maze of tiny streets around the Old Harbour area of Chania. (hard 'ch' and accent on the 'ia,' pronounced "ya") I had booked a room close to the harbour because I imagined that his ship would have been docked nearby and that he might have come to know the area around the port. Eventually my driver stopped at the end of an alley with a no entry sign. "Must walk – is no cars - Ifigenia just here. This closest way."

I trundled my flight bag, its wheels clattering along the cobblestones and thought of the architect/designer William

115

McDonough saying that man's slow progress in the world is indicated by the hundreds of years it has taken to put wheels under our luggage. Thump, thump went the wheels in the silence of the deserted lane. I was transported into a film set for The Merchant of Venice – tall mansions with layers of shuttered windows and wrought iron balconies in the hooded darkness. I eventually called out: "Ifigenia" with the correct Greek inflections. Immediately there was an answering cry: "Down here." So I followed the voice and was greeted at the immense door of a mansion by another Greek Al Pacino look-alike who showed me to my room in an annex mansion round the corner. A four-poster bed with elegant lace curtains dominated the room. On a side table were two glasses, a bottle of wine and a bottle hand-labeled "Raki" I am going to need that, I thought, as the cold breezed around me. Al Pacino switched on a heater situated high up near the lofty ceiling. Shakespearean it was. And frigid. The heater made little appreciable difference even after I had fortified myself with the fiery Raki. The heater stayed on at full blast throughout my two days in Chania.

*We got up anchor the next morning and steamed round to a place called Suda Bay. A picnic party was arranged aboard the ship for a trip into the interior of the island. The party embarked aboard some eighteen brakes at Suda Bay and a drive of ten miles through very English looking scenery brought us to the foot of a range of hills away behind the town of Chania. A halt was made here for lunch at a garden attached to an hostelry kept by a Greek, the find drive having whetted our appetites to a remarkable degree. The garden, in which were many orange and lemon trees bearing fruit, was raided for an impromptu dessert which foray entailed about half an hours heated discussion and incidentally a payment of a few shillings to mollify the irate proprietor.*

*The whole party was then formed up, under the leadership of our Greek guide, and a start made to ascend one of the higher mountains. Before long the party had tailed off to a string about half a mile long and I noticed a few sneaking back towards the plain (and the commissariat wagon) before we had really made a start. About half way up a halt was made for a spell and to collect forces, and to decide whither we should continue the ascent. The minority of which I was one, decided to reach the top the majority preferring to rest until we returned. The guide had made the pace pretty warm in the first half, and as they lay sweating on the gorse I was reminded of a scene from "The Hunt" in Scott's "Lady of the Lake" where he says "So shrewdly on the mountain side, had the bold burst their mettle tried". A stiff climb brought us to the top, but we were amply repaid by the magnificent view obtained. Looking towards the interior was a deep fertile valley and beyond that towered the snow-capped mountains that I have mentioned previously in this book.*

*Of course I have seen snow-capped mountains galore and thought nothing of them, but to see oranges and lemons ripening in the valley below and then to glance upwards to the white peaks gives a contrast that can never be seen in our own zone. Towards the sea, from which we were divided by the wide plain we had driven through earlier in the day, we could discern to the right the ships in Suda Bay like miniatures in a kaleidoscope. The town of Chania with its rich, warm colouring lay right on our front and to the left stretched a rugged coastline with many small hamlets perched here and there where-ever a bit of soil warranted cultivation. The descent didn't give us much trouble and having picked up the remainder of our party, we proceeded back to the garden of our Greek host for tea.*

*The keen mountain air had made us hungry as hunters and the amount of bread and butter and "pussers" jam we tucked away surprised some of ourselves. We then formed up for the drive home which was by way of Chania and back by the main road to Suda Bay, which was reached about seven in the evening. We returned aboard quite sun-browned and tired and turned in with the feeling that we had spent a most enjoyable day and personally I felt much better for the delightful change. Two Russian and one French ship lay with us at Suda and a good deal of fraternizing took place among the officers and men, especially between the English and French. Well, well! Fraternizing today and probably cutting one another up for mincemeat tomorrow at the bidding of our respective Capitalist friends, but as I might have to take an active part in the next squabble I refrain from following further such a painful subject.*

I fell asleep under the warm quilt thinking about my plan to relive grandfather's experience of the climb and the views from the peak. I was determined to find the spot and see the panorama for myself. Perhaps the hotel staff could help me locate it from his description. In the frosty morning I found my way to the main mansion, which had a sign over the door: "Hotel Vassilis." I met Captain Vassilis, who owned both properties, in the lobby. He was a stocky, barrel-chested man with a full head of dark, wavy hair and craggy features which had clearly been too much in the sun and the wind. Although he told me that he had little English, he had enough to tell me that he had been a sea captain like his father; he pointed to a

118

full length portrait on the wall beside us. The hotel was named for his father. "Canada good country, Port of Montreal I have been to." When I started to ask for directions to the peak he brushed my questions aside: "Wait, my daughter, good English." After a few minutes she arrived. In complete contrast to her burly father she was small, slim and blonde. She had a good grasp of what I wanted after I had read out the relevant sections of the journal. "Your great father was Royal Navy", said Vassilis, "we help you." They conferred in Greek then Xanthe (the daughter) told me that I must go to the village of Malaxa because grandfather's description fitted the hills near there. Her father agreed. Xanthe, who seemed to be the person running the hotel, offered to find me a rental car and the maps for finding Malaxa.

After some high priced alternatives she found me a company which rented me a rather battered Daewoo minibox and I set off with a road map and a prayer. The Daewoo and I snaked up the 16k mountain road which barely had any traffic – a contrast to the crowded major roads and the busy towns. When I stopped for a break from the endless hairpin bends there was silence. Only the sound of birdsong and goat bells tinkling from the cliffs. Around Malaxa I tried various trails and tracks leading up the hillside. Nothing led anywhere. Just beyond the village I came to a crossroads where the main road went straight ahead and a rough road went up to the left. I felt a strange urge which led me to take the uphill track. Soon it became rough and boulder-strewn; I decided that only a 4x4 could make it. I parked the minibox and continued the climb on foot. On my right was a tiny chapel complete with a glassed-in shrine on the road. I remembered the pre-Christian custom of placing the first fruits of the harvest in such boxes. It also contained a silver replica of a saint. By contrast, below the chapel was a non-ancient tire dump. In the distance I could see the snowy mountains he described and the citrus trees in the valley below.

After half an hour's steady climb I began to anticipate Grandfather's view round each succeeding bend. I could almost hear my little boy voice asking plaintively: "When are we going to get there?" I imagined Grandfather saying; "Just keep going and you will reach the view." Eventually I saw that the track was a service road for a group of microwave pylons I could see in the distance and realized that the only vehicle that had gone past must be connected with that complex. Then I rounded a bend about 200 metres from the first pylon and there it was; the view just as grandfather had described it. I saw a ferry in the blue waters of Souda Bay, the warm brown colours of Chania ahead and the rugged grey coastline to the left. The peak he reached was blocked off by a wire fence surrounding the masts. Yet the view was just as he described it a hundred years ago. I learned another life lesson from grandfather's encouraging voice in my head: Don't give up easily; pursue your goal no matter what obstacles you encounter or how discouraged you feel. As a friend remarked: "Discipline is doing what you set out to do even when you don't feel like doing it."

## CHAPTER 7: COTE D'AZURE AND MENORCA

*The unveiling of memorials in Nice to the late Queen Victoria and in Cannes to King Edward VII together with the usual pomp and pageantry common to these ceremonies demanded our presence in the south of France. We left the Grand Harbour in Valetta, Malta on the evening of Good Friday and, with a sea as smooth as glass, we had a splendid passage to our destination. We arrived at Golfe-Juan on the Riviera on Monday forenoon and anchored in the bay alongside the 1ˢᵗ sea squadron of the French Fleet. We were within easy distance of all the famous watering places, where the aristocrats of Europe and the millionaire meat packers and pork Kings of America come to spend their surplus wealth, and I might mention that a good many of the latter have more than will allow them to pass "The eye of the needle test" demanded by Jamie.*

*The statue to Queen Victoria was unveiled at Nice on Friday the 12ᵗʰ of April, the French and British sailors forming the guard of honour*

I based myself in Barcelona so as to follow grandfather's travels to the Riviera and to the island of Menorca. By the time I unpacked in my hotel bedroom I realized that I was desperately short of clean clothes. The Greek islands, Athens and Delphi had been such a whirlwind of grandfather places and sight-seeing that clothes had simply accumulated in my main suitcase while I lived out of my backpack. I needed a laundry. The hotel prices were outrageous so I asked the clerk at the desk about laundromats.

121

She did not understand what I was talking about until I mentioned the words "washer and drier."

"Oh, we have very few in Espana; most people have their own – only one I know is far from here."

She gave me directions using the sketchy hotel map so I took the subway to the stop she indicated with a ballpoint circle and asked the way. Fortunately a passer-by gave me the name of a grimy little side street and I saw the sign with a picture of a washer. By contrast with the street the interior was spotless and full of gleaming machines. The only problem was that the directions were in Spanish and there was no attendant to direct me. No other customers either. I stood facing the window onto the street feeling utterly helpless. An elderly woman saw me, came in and said something like "Non comprehendo?" I comprehended all right and with the help of sign language she showed me exactly how to operate both washer and drier. She ensured that I had the right change, wished me well and left. She had not come in to do a load of laundry herself but simply to help a bemused foreigner.

Not only was Barcelona by reputation a fabulous city which I had never visited but it was a hub for a local Mediterranean airline. I booked a flight from Barcelona to Nice, which would give me easy access to both Cannes and Monaco. My arrival time at Nice Airport was 22.40 where I was to collect a car and drive 12 kilometers to my accommodation at Villa Saint-Exupery on the outskirts of the city. I chose the Villa on the internet because it was close to the coastal autoroute and had high ratings from the hostel association. Besides Saint Exupery's book, *The Little Prince*, is one of my favourites.

A few nights before my flight, I began to have doubts about the arrangements involving the rental car. I lost sleep imagining arriving after midnight and trying to get to the Villa in the dark on an unfamiliar autoroute. In the sober light of day I recalled my grandfather's enlistment in the navy despite his dislike of the sea and ships and warfare. He had the courage to overcome his fears and doubts in order to support his young family. I had a sense that he was helping me put my fears to rest.

It turned out that my dread-filled fantasies were partially fulfilled when I arrived in Nice. It so happened that I was the last passenger to disembark from the aircraft. All the others had left by the time I walked across the tarmac to the single-storey terminal, which was deserted except for a desultory cleaner. When I eventually found the Budget rental desk a sign announced that Budget had merged with Avis. Next to the "Closed" sign at the Avis rental desk a small sign read: "After Hours at Terminal 2." So this was Terminal 1. The solitary female cleaner was able to decipher my fractured French and directed me to the shuttle bus, which dropped me off outside Terminal 2, where I headed in the direction of the parking garage and the rental companies. It was a long walk but finally I was behind the wheel of a new Renault with a complicated set of written directions to the Villa on the seat beside me. The Avis clerk's emphasis on the fact that it was a new car added to my nervousness, as I drove cautiously from the airport and onto the autoroute, ignoring as best as I could the honking cars behind me. Steep streets, one way systems and the directions barely readable in the dark made the short distance to the Villa seem endless, but eventually I found my way. Fortunately there was very little traffic in suburbia at 2 AM. With a huge sense of relief I parked the Renault in the tiny lot of the Villa and was greeted by a slim young

Frenchman called Georges, who introduced himself as the night manager. My troubles were not quite over because Georges was unable to unlock the room I had been allocated with the plastic Little Prince card he had. After three trips back to the office he finally found a 4-person room which was unlocked, apologized profusely and assured me that all would be sorted out in the morning. Never mind, I said, and slept soundly in my bunk bed that night.

Morning brought a cheerier light on things. The yellow-painted corridors were decorated with Impressionist prints and the direction signs were illustrated with cute Little Prince drawings. The ground-floor restaurant had been the chapel of the former monastery and served a great "all you can eat" breakfast with fruit, twelve different cereals, fresh baguettes and urns of coffee. Guests sat at refectory tables chatting; most were young but there were some grey panthers like me. The room was lit by skylights; on the open balconies above I could see people clicking away on a bank of computers. Free wireless internet was also available throughout the building for those like me with their own laptops. Stained-glass windows behind the refectory tables preserved the monastic look of the room and a massive bar with a kitchen behind it dominated one wall. After breakfast, which was included in the reasonable room charge, I walked round the park-like garden with its olive trees and pines, admiring the pastel Provencal-style building. Friendly staff sorted out the door-lock problem and I stowed my laptop and the contents of my airline bag in my monastic single bedroom where I was to spend the next three nights after my day trips to Cannes and Monte Carlo.

The search in Nice for the statue of Queen Victoria began with Google, which yielded both the street address and

124

the appropriate bus route. She stands in front of the opulent Hotel Regina in an area of Nice called Cimiez where the street names are all English. The name of the sculptor, Louis Maubert, is carved unobtrusively into the pedestal dated 1912, exactly as grandfather's diary says. I felt a certain thrill at the thought that he had been there for her unveiling, standing to attention with the other sailors as part of the guard of honour. The queen smiles down at five animated young girls presenting her with garlands of flowers, an image rather in contrast with the stiff formality of her other monuments that I had seen. It seems she enjoyed her visits to Cimiez in the latter years of her reign, staying in a suite built for her in the Regina Hotel. That place has since been converted to offices and private apartments, a belle-epoque building that however retains the name. But she would have known it as L'Excelsior Regina Palace.

Cimiez has been a district for the elite since Roman times; a short way up the slope from Victoria's statue are the ruins of ancient Roman baths and an amphitheatre alongside a seventeenth-century villa that now houses the Matisse museum. During the period known as La Belle Époque (approximately 1870 – 1914) sun-seeking visitors and retired Brits built stylish mansions rising up the hill dominated by the Regina at the summit. Matisse lived in the hotel at various times. Now most of the mansions have been subdivided or turned into stylish offices. Cimiez is still Nice's most luxurious quarter.

Having had my fill of the site, I followed signs to the Matisse museum, which is inside a leafy park with a grove of olive trees. Interestingly, the little streets leading up to it were named after famous American jazz artists: Allee Duke Ellington and Allee Miles Davis, for example. In the park itself to my delight I found handsome busts of Louis Armstrong and Lionel Hampton. Why the memorials to artists who happen to be some of my favourite musicians, I wondered? The guidebook said that the park and the Roman Amphitheatre were venues for the annual Nice Jazz Festival. The lady at the check-in counter at the museum turned haughty when I expressed astonishment that there was no charge for entry. "All our museums in Nice are free," she said with a sniff. The villa was bought and restored by the city in the 1960's to house a fabulous collection of Matisse's works – paintings, sculptures and gouache cutouts. His own possessions, letters and photographs give remarkable insights into his life and times.

Five kilometers from the museum down the Boulevard de Cimiez walking in the direction of the sea, I found myself in a tangle of alleys and twisted walkways. It felt like a dockside area bursting with busy life. The high buildings with balconies and clotheslines were painted in pastel colours - yellow, ochre, orange and pink. Spires and domes of baroque churches thrust up from among the red tiled roofs of the houses. The streets were lined with boutiques, selling clothing and jewellery, tiny cafes, and tattoo parlours. Pavement artists were busy at work, sketching tourists or touting for customers. This district dates back to the 18th century and is now known as Vieux Nice. The winding, narrow streets opened into compact squares, in one of which I discovered the famous fruit and flower market referred to in the guidebook. Unfortunately it closed at 1.00 pm; I was too late - workmen were busy spraying the cobbles with hoses. Strolling further south I found myself at the Promenade des Anglais, which stretches along the seafront for 7 kilometers. The curve of the bay was spectacular as were the crowds of elegantly dressed walkers. My guidebook told me that the promenade reflected the 18th century invasion by visitors, invalids, and gamblers, seeking money or sun or prestige or all three. I walked west along the seafront and discovered the old harbour which was tiny. Behind the breakwater constructed from huge stones piled against a concrete wall were a smattering of opulent cigarette boats and humble looking sailboats. From here I caught a bus to Villefranche-sur-Mer where HMS Lancaster had anchored offshore. The wide bay looked tranquil as a mirror in the late afternoon sun with tethered sailboats in the foreground against a backdrop of the tiny town nestled into the cliffs. I couldn't help but see the three-funnelled Lancaster reflected from the bay, belching thick dark smoke. I swept my gaze round the bay: a well-protected anchorage, as grandfather had observed. I went back to the city centre by bus and then by streetcar out to the Villa.

*We left Golfe-Juan on Sunday forenoon meeting the escorting cruisers of the French Fleet outside, and steamed in company to Villa-France Bay which was to be our last port of call and where we arrived at noon. While here I visited the romantic town of Monte Carlo and was so delighted and charmed with everything I saw that I would like to give a less fortunate reader a detailed description of the world's greatest gambling den. Like a shining jewel on the border of the azure sea, in a rich setting of pine clad mountains, picturesque coast scenery and beautiful gardens, stands Monte Carlo and its world-famed casino, possessing all the subtle and elusive charm of romance. Indeed, there is no spot in the whole of Europe that is so full of romance, and has witnessed such tragedy, pathos and emotion as Monte Carlo, without question the gayest and greatest gambling den in the world.*

Just now the casino authorities and the hotel proprietors are happy for the Monte Carlo season is in full swing. More people go to Monte Carlo now than ever did before so there is more play and consequently more money is lost. The difference is that roulette is now being played by the public generally, and not by a few special gamblers, and it follows upon that that there is more silver seen on the tables than formerly, when it was all gold and notes, and also the display of dress is less brilliant.

The romance of Monte Carlo lies in its remarkable history and the fortunes that have been lost and made on the spin of a wheel, and tragedy in the suicides' graveyard, high up on a barren hillside, some distance from the road. You may visit Monte Carlo a dozen times and never see it for it is hid from the public gaze. A little over thirty years ago the place was a bare rocky desert. The peasants eked out a scanty livelihood by cultivating their vineyards and olive woods, their poverty being increased by the exactions of each succeeding Prince of Monaco, who turned every industry into a state monopoly and lived by the labour of the people. When first built the casino contained nothing of the art treasures, the mirrors and gildings that ornament the building of today, and consisted solely of the Atrium, a gambling room and a reading room. In order to people this arid desert, those employed to exploit the Casino actually offered free land to anyone who could build villas and hotels thereon but the offer was refused, and the land once to be had for nothing is today of priceless value.

The gaming and concert rooms of the Casino are marvels of profuse decoration and the concert room is remarkable for its painted ceiling, which is the work of four celebrated painters. Access is easily obtainable to the gaming *saloons. All one has to do is to present their visiting card at one counter when the clerk hands you the necessary permit that passes you through. The same formality has to be gone through every time you enter. This season there are twelve roulette tables in full swing, and at any time of the day almost anywhere from a score to fifty people can be seen at each. The only other game played at Monte Carlo is trente-et-quarante, a card game.*

*Everyone has heard of the game of roulette which consists of the spinning of a wheel in a tray and the sending of a white marble ball in the opposite direction. The tray is numbered 1 to 36 and 0, and the winning number is that in which the ball finally rests. If you back the winning number you receive thirty five times your stake. Or you can back two numbers, and if one turns up you receive seventeen times your stake, and so on. The smallest coin you can put down is 5 francs, the limit being 240 pounds. Obviously, the chances are thirty six to one against any one number turning up. So none but the reckless gambler takes one number at a time. He backs twelve, or takes evens, namely; places his money on red or black or takes the numbers above or below eighteen. He endeavours to work by "a system". At a kiosk not a hundred yards from the casino you can buy an "infallible method of winning" for five francs. Of course were it really infallible its sale would soon be suppressed. Nevertheless it is common knowledge that people have made huge fortunes by playing according to systems. There is the case of "Monte Carlo Wells" who won 60,000 pounds. It was but two years ago that Mr. Huntley Walker left the casino 16,000 the richer after playing according to a system which he declares took him fifteen years to perfect. Five years ago, an immensely wealthy American, Colonel Powell, the owner of mines in Mexico, won 40,000 pounds. This season a German gentleman won 20,000 and prudently retired, while I heard of numerous small wins. But in spite of all these huge sums which have been won, the bank holds its own against all systems, plungers and persevering gamblers and, as a witty proverb invented in the days of M. Blanc, the founder of the casino, truly says, "The black often loses, and red often loses, but white (Blanc) always wins" and his winnings range from one million to one and a half million every year.*

*Monte Carlo itself may be described as a delightful little resort of hotels, fashionable villas, and jewellers' shops in the midst of flower gardens. The gardens attached to the casino itself are unquestionably one of the finest sights of the Riviera. They are always a blaze of colour. Then there is the Oceanographic Museum erected by the Prince of Monaco (who by the way is an expert on this matter and was delivering a lecture in Vienna while I was there) and a magnificent cathedral. The latter was built by money obtained from gamblers, and the Bishop and staff of priests are all paid from the profits made at the casino. The casino, too, pays all the taxes; in fact virtually runs the place.*

*There is one spot however which the casino authorities and the police in its pay wish visitors to avoid, and this is the suicides' graveyard. It is certainly a distressing spot, surrounded by high solid walls situated high up on a barren hillside. There is no road to it and not one person in every ten who visit the casino has seen it. Entrance is gained to it by an iron gate which is always kept locked. Peeping in, a melancholy sight meets the eye. It has not the slightest resemblance to an ordinary graveyard. It is dirty and neglected; rank, half-shrivelled grass grows up through stones and sand; there are no monuments and no mounds. The graves are all quite flat. One of them only has a lining of tiles round it, and the remains of a wooden cross at its head. Others are merely marked by a tiny piece of wood, about a foot high, and marked only by a number. Here and there are the remains of broken wreaths. Should a person commit suicide in the casino grounds or at his hotel, and has taken the precaution, as is usual in such cases, to leave no trace of his identity, this is the spot to which he is taken in the dead of night and secretly and quietly buried. Such is the mixture of romance and realism which constitutes the charm of Monte Carlo -that laughing, enchanting garden of earth, which art and nature have combined to render perfect, and which yet is but a snare for many who are ignorant of the fatal plague shots hidden beneath its loveliness. But the place is always alluring, for its charm is ever new and the leafless, ashy grey rock, rising two thousand feet above the small, verdure-clothed, sun kissed town gives dignity and majesty to the surrounding so immutable and changeless in the midst of changing things. To give a slight idea of the attractions outside the casino; on a Sunday afternoon I was there I saw the finish of a marathon race, the finish of a motor boat race (which was won by the Duke of Westminster's boat) and a hydro-aeroplane taking passengers for 10 pounds a flight. The latter is quite new and has been the hit of the season here, being largely patronized by the wealthy visitor on the outlook for new sensations.*

The following morning it was raining when I swung the Renault from the coastal autoroute onto the exit ramp to Monte Carlo. Traffic was slow, which was helpful, for I was feeling my way down the steep descent, map at the ready. To my relief there was a parking garage just as I entered the town. I parked and oriented myself at the pedestrian exit, where a

131

police officer told me that the graveyard was next to the hospital. He directed me to a nearby building which turned out to contain a large elevator down to various levels of the steep town. The shelter was welcome because the light rain had become a steady downpour. At the appropriate level I followed signs for the Princess Grace Hospital and, after walking past it, I found the cemetery. It was carved into the steep hillside with terraces, each about eight feet wide and eighty feet long. Gazing down from the topmost terrace I realized that the terraces were in fact arranged in a continuous sloping zig-zag down to the lower wall at the road. The wind and rain turned taking photographs into a hazardous balancing act. I explored all the terraces from the main entrance at the top downward. They were tightly packed with tombstones, memorials, marble steps and floor tiles, columns, crosses, framed photographs, urns, angels, flower boxes and sarcophaguses. There was no sign of the suicides' graveyard grandfather so vividly described.

But at one corner of the lowest terrace there was an area about the size of a king-size bed filled with pebbles. Leaning against the inside of the wall facing the street were two decaying wooden stakes about a foot high, each with a tin tag inscribed with a year and a number. One was dated 1896 number 10, the other 1897 number 11. Yellow wild flowers filled the bed. These then were two of the grave markers grandfather described. Below the terrace was a wall at right angles to the street, separating the ornate cemetery from a gravel car park. I climbed down to it and found that the entrance here was flanked by two pillars with a metal gate hanging from one. I saw that the wall along the street had been torn down in this section and replaced with a rickety wooden fence. Portions of the old stone wall were still standing. Eureka! This was the suicide graveyard. The ornate iron gates and the remains of the high wall fitted grandfather's description. I could see that it had originally been walled on all four sides. Presumably the authorities required extra space for a car park so the suicides' remains must have been gathered together and buried in the bed of pebbles immediately above.

Mission accomplished, I could now explore the city which Somerset Maugham once described as "a sunny place for shady people." Today was not sunny and with all the raingear it was difficult to pick out the shady people. I walked down the steep streets, amazed at the succession of huge plate glass windows filled with exotic cars. The dealerships were vast. Next there were luxury clothing and jewellery shops with a constant swish of limousine tires churning up the wet roads alongside. By now I was wet too; my umbrella could not cope with the gusts of wind and the driving rain. As I walked toward the casino for which Monte Carlo is famous, the rain changed to sleet mixed with flakes of snow. The vast portal gave way into a lobby which seemed to go on for ever. Mirrors everywhere. At the ticket office I showed my passport, paid ten euros and was admitted to the first of three salons. The permit allowed me to walk around but not to gamble; for that I would have had to pay extra. I took in the sumptuous sofas, the mahogany furnishings in dark reds, the rich formal paintings, knots of players around tables. All much as grandfather described except for the flock of slot machines in garish rows, some operated feverishly, perhaps desperately, others more casually by bored-looking patrons. I wished I had a spy camera to record the gamblers' emotions or the concealing of expressions in a tight-lipped mask. By regulation, my camera had been checked in at the entrance.

As I emerged from the casino, unfurling my umbrella, I saw a sight before me startlingly reminiscent of home,

133

Canada. The lavish tropical gardens were covered with fresh white snow, coating the palm leaves and wedged in the cactus leaves. An excited doorman told me that both the bus service and the autoroute had been shut down and that cars were sliding everywhere. "I have never seen snow here in my life," said his colleague. The sky was dark; more snow was on the way. I slip-slided my way back towards my car. It was a long uphill hike but it gave me time to think about the city of Monte Carlo and the Kingdom of Monaco, which has been ruled by the Grimaldi family since the 13$^{th}$ century, making it the oldest monarchy in Europe. The entire country is roughly the size of High Park in Toronto. Monte Carlo is hemmed in between the Mediterranean and the coastal mountains. As a result, construction cranes are busy all along the skyline building ever higher skyscrapers, there being nowhere to expand but upwards. Eventually I found the parking garage with my car. The journey back to Nice took over three hours of stop-start driving. It had taken me just twenty minutes to get there in the morning. I decided that the car was unnecessary because trains and buses were both inexpensive and convenient. So when I reached Nice I drove to the airport and returned the car. I had already established from the villa's information package that I could take a train to Cannes the next day and then an airport shuttle bus from there for my red-eye flight back to Barcelona.

I awoke the next morning with sunlight streaming into my bedroom. Outside the window in the Villa garden the tropical trees and shrubs were laden with snow, the sunlight sparkling off the misty crystals. Later as I took the train to Cannes only vestiges of the snow remained alongside the track, but the sound of dripping melt persisted.

*Early on the morning of the 13th April the fleets steamed round to Cannes for the unveiling ceremony of the statue of King Edward VII. The statue was unveiled amidst a scene of great enthusiasm as the late King was a welcome and popular visitor when he came to the Riviera. The total height of the memorial is over twenty feet. The statue itself, of marble, represents the King in yachting costume, telescope in hand, near the wheel of the yacht Britannia. The bronze reliefs on the pedestal depict the "Regatta fetes at Cannes", "The Battle of Flowers", and a female figure (symbolic of the town of Cannes) seated amidst olives, the branches of which she gathers, and distributes broad cast, the feet of the figure being laved by the blue waters of the Mediterranean.*

In Cannes my search for the statue of King Edward VII proved much more difficult than for Queen Victoria in Nice. No one at the tourist offices could help. I decided to visit the casinos because an old postcard on the internet depicted Edward in naval uniform standing in front of a casino. (There are four casinos in Cannes.) No sign of his statue. Then I had a brainwave: the municipal casino near the docks was a likely venue. Sure enough one of the docks was named Jetee Albert-Edouard. The king had been named Albert after his father but took the name Edward when he ascended the throne for fear of the British public's hostility to his father's German connection. The area beside the dock was covered with a sprawling new Palais de Festivals ("ugly as a misplaced missile silo" according to the Rough Guide) that incorporated a casino. Confirmation that I had indeed come upon the site of the old statue came from the Cannes Office of Cultural Affairs. There I learnt that the statue had been demolished to make way for the festival site. Apparently it had been in poor condition. It must not have been carved from the same stone as his mother's memorial. Ironically he did not last nearly as long on the British throne as she had.

The concrete "missile silo" stands between the harbour and the beach and marks one end of the Promenade de la Croisette - "Riviera's most glamorous seafront" according to my guidebook. The curving beach stretches two and a half kilometers from the festival site to the Point at the end of the bay. Along the wide boulevard facing the beach are pricy shops and swanky hotels. The most prestigious place to stay during the summer film festival is the Carlton. It is where movie deals are made and it is a haunt of the top movie stars; Grace Kelly made arrangements to meet Prince Rainier here for a photo shoot which led to their eventual marriage. It was the main location for her film with Cary Grant, *To Catch a Thief* directed by Alfred Hitchcock. With its elaborate, carved pillars and balconies, the hotel looks like a large square wedding cake with creamy pink icing. The domes at each seafront corner are reputed to have been inspired by the breasts of a famous World War 1 courtesan.

This playground for the rich and famous was once a fishing village until it was "discovered" in the 1830's by Lord Brougham, an ex-British Chancellor of the Exchequer, who could not get to Nice because of a cholera epidemic. So he settled for Cannes and built a mansion there for his summer holidays. A contingent of English aristocrats and people with money followed suit. Cannes' architecture is less Italianate than that in Nice; it is more Provencal. Frowning down on all the frivolity is a church on the hill facing the Old Port. I climbed up a series of circuitous cobbled lanes to the top of the hill. The church - l'Eglise Notre Dame d'Esperance- looks benign rather than disapproving up close. Constructed in the 17th century, its doors and windows are rectangular rather than ornate arched Gothic. The tower has a prominent clock on all four sides. The colour is pink ochre; it struck me as warm and friendly. One travel writer describes the church as having the look of a Provencal farmhouse; the tiled red roof bears out that description. At the opposite end of what is a craggy outcrop of rock is a ruined castle, only its tower still standing. The view from the castle gardens is spectacular – the harbour entrance with the open sea beyond; the Old Port with a forest of sailboat masts and then the sweeping promenade and the beach.

*We left our anchorage at Villa France at 9 o'clock on Wednesday evening and just after ten all we had to remind us of our pleasant stay on the Riviera was the last glimpse of the twinkling lights of Nice over our starboard quarter as we turned our bows towards the land of goats and holystones.*

## MAHON, MENORCA

After two days' sightseeing in Barcelona I flew to the island of Menorca. It is the northernmost of the four Balearic Islands which are administered by Spain. The capital, Port Mahon (Mahon in Spanish, Mao in Catalan), was a Royal Navy base from 1708 to 1802. At the airport tourist office I was greeted by a clerk with a strong Manchester accent. I asked if he was English. No, but his father was from Manchester and had married a local girl after the war. I discovered that many local people spoke with English accents, also products of mixed marriages. According to a rental agent I met, the island is still a popular destination for British tourists, many of whom come here to retire.

137

*Leave was granted at Port Mahon for the afternoon and I went ashore with a few of my fellow sufferers for a walk and a look round. We found the natives very industrious working mostly in their own homes, making boots and chain purses. The latter is very tedious work and is done by women and young girls and the strain on the eyes is so great that they rapidly become short sighted. There are few factories, the family working together at home, and taking the finished articles to a capitalist who supplies them with raw material and pays them a miserable pittance for their labour. The English had this island in their possession and although they vacated it 100 years ago, the traces of their occupation can still be seen in the dress and language of the people.*

The city and the harbour are situated at the end of a seven-kilometer-long inlet gashed into the eastern side of the island. The port is still regarded as one of the safest havens for ships in the Mediterranean, the steep cliffs affording protection from fierce storms. On my first morning I followed the cliff top hike from my hotel, near the centre, to the mouth of the inlet, which gave me splendid views of the town's historical sites and villages below. The walking guide gave details of the sights along the way. At the starting point was the pentagon-shaped island, Isla de Pinto, with the whitewashed Royal Navy Arsenal built in the precise lines of neo-classical Georgian style. Red-tiled roofs peeped out from a series of large fir trees covering much of the substantial building. Prominent over the rooftops was an ornate clock tower in the style of those in English private schools like Eton or Harrow. It was intricate in design with Gothic clerestory

138

windows, clock faces on all four sides and an elaborate helmet-shaped dome complete with spike at the top. Lawns led down to a low whitewashed wall at the blue water's edge. A closer look with binoculars revealed barrels of cannons protruding unobtrusively from the sea wall.

Further along the walk my guidebook told me to look out for a red house with a prominent façade facing the water. "Legend has it," it said, "that the lovers Lord Nelson and Lady Hamilton stayed there." There it was across the inlet; red brick walls with windows and doors framed in white and a tower at one end. The façade had imposing white pillars in the classical Georgian style that I find so attractive. Stone steps led down from the garden to the dock, where, presumably in 1799, a fleet-looking sailboat awaited, ready to whisk the admiral back to his flagship if need be. I walked on past other features listed in the guidebook: elegant summer houses with discreet swimming docks beneath them, a large hospital and the separate French and English cemeteries. Looking back towards the east end of the city I was struck with how white it appeared against the dark forest on the hills behind.

The bays on both shores of the inlet contained marinas with many masts and motor boats. Near the mouth of one pretty bay was a fishing village named Calesfont. It was time for lunch. There was a brisk breeze blowing but it was sunny so I chose a table on the deserted roof patio of a cafe overlooking the water. From the parapet I had a clear view of boats of the vessels moored below. Some were little fishing boats, others were runabouts. One end of each was fastened to the dock, the other to a colourful buoy some distance out in the water. The buoys were like balloons decorating the curve of the little bay. I peered over the edge of the parapet and saw a larger fishing boat moored immediately below me. The boat

139

itself was shabby; battered here and there and in need of a coat of paint. However on deck it was a different story; I saw five carefully rolled sets of nets, a stack of trays for fish and neat coils of rope on the cabin roof. The little vessel had an air of preparedness about her as though she was anticipating the tasks at hand. I could hear the cries of seagulls swooping and soaring over her stern, perhaps expecting a meal of discarded fish parts. I could smell the tangy mix of salt air, ozone and fish. While I waited for my lunch I thought about my grandfather's distaste for all things connected with boats and the sea. I reflected on my fascination with water and with ships both large and small. What a difference between us! Perhaps his negative feelings were based on his enforced enlistment in the navy and his opposition to war. In any event his focus was on the family he had to support rather than his own antipathy.

Some ten or twelve feet back from the dock was a row of single-storey shops, tavernas and outdoor patios strung along the curve. A mosaic of paving stones covered the intervening area. Superimposed above the shops was a street with larger two and three storey buildings which looked as though they were growing out of the rooftops below. I could pick out hotels, rooming houses, apartments and stores. In contrast to the whitewashed buildings below, the upper row were painted in pastel colours: cream, pale pink, light blue and maroon.

After a delicious lunch of fresh cod fillet I continued to follow the cliff top trail. Across the inlet were the gaping windows of a derelict military hospital built by the English on Isla del Rei. The English named it Bloody Island. At the next town - Es Castell – I was surprised to see the streets laid out with geometric precision, many with English names. The

140

houses looked Georgian in style but with a Mediterranean twist—instead of grey stone the walls were stucco painted in light shades, the windows and doors outlined in white. The base and the eaves were also painted white. According to the map, the town had been laid out during the British occupation in 1771 and named Georgetown after George III. The central square had been a parade ground with a military headquarters on one side. The building, a very handsome maroon with green shutters and white-trimmed windows and doors was now home to the city hall and a military museum. On one side of the square was a restaurant with outdoor tables and umbrellas. In front of the tables a game of bocce was in progress using the smoothed-out gravel as a pitch. The men who played it wore intent faces, and some of them would finish off their shots with a rather amusing pirouette .

*We witnessed a football match between the "Bacchantes" team and a team picked in the town. There was not any marked superiority on either side, although the sailors ran out winners in the end. We next visited the church of Santa Maria where an organ recital was being given in honour of the visit of the fleet. This organ is noted as being the oldest and one of the biggest in the world and really it was a beautiful instrument and well worth seeing.*

The next day was a Saturday and I rented a bicycle and rode towards the football stadium grandfather talks about from which the shouts of the crowds got louder as I approached. A match between two island teams was in progress; I stood with the vociferous supporters of the local team just behind the touchline as the ball was swept from one end of the field to the

141

other. I felt a thrill of recognition that grandfather had watched his shipmates play on this very ground all those years ago. I wondered whether he enjoyed football; I know that his sons (my uncles) were keen cricketers when I first met them in their thirties. I never played football as a schoolboy since rugby and cricket were the national games in South Africa. However, I do like to watch the clever tactics in football and this game was enjoyable for that reason.

I had established which of the three central churches was home to the organ grandfather heard – Santa Maria - and decided to attend both masses the following day to maximize my chances of hearing the organ. The first mass was in Spanish and began at 11 am. I wondered how I could record the music when it struck me that my camera records sound. So I got to the service in good time, sat about halfway back where there were few people and unzipped my camera from its case. When I held the camera up to my eye I was horrified to read a message that there was no memory card; I had left it on the table next to my computer at the hotel. I decided to come back to the mass at 7. I slipped out while the strains of the opening hymn were being played on the enormous organ. I returned in the evening and readied myself for the mass in Catalan. This time there was no error message. The organ began to play a prelude which I guessed was Bach. I was ready with the camera and panned slowly over the sumptuous ceiling and the arches of the Gothic church founded in 1287. When the priest and his acolytes emerged from a side door, I filmed them making their way up the sets of steps to the altar. The organ concluded the Bach prelude as the priest bowed low. I was close to tears, touched by the image of my grandfather in his best uniform listening to the same instrument a hundred years before. I shut my eyes as the organist led into the opening hymn; I could almost sense the presence of those British sailors and their gratitude at being given special entertainment.

The organ towers 45 meters over the arched entrance at the back of the church. The 3506 pipes are arranged in three rows surmounted by a crowned statue in gold with a shield in the left hand and an orb in the right. I assumed he represented God, set so high that he is immediately beneath the decorated ceiling. On each side of the topmost row are angels framed in gold, one holding clashing cymbals the other a drum. Two gold urns complete the row. Above the row is inscribed "LAUDATE DOMINUM" (Praise to God) with it's completion beneath: "IN CHORDIS E ORGANO" (in chords from the organ). More gold winged figures and cherubs adorn the second and third layers of pipes. The organ is 9 meters wide and has four keyboards. It was built in Barcelona and decorated by a Menorcan sculptor. The date inscribed at the base is 1810.

At the front of the church is the high altar also heavily decorated in gold. Four columns above the altar table enclose a sculpture of Jesus on the cross. Soaring above him and far larger is a statue of Mary, her head surmounted with a circle of blue and white stars. Her hands are outstretched in a welcoming gesture and she is surrounded by twelve figures in gold - angels, cherubs and saints. The ceiling is criss-crossed with arches and decorated with paintings. Down each side of the nave are tiny chapels dedicated to different saints.

On my way back to the hotel I wheeled my bike past a long colonnade stretching across the side of a plaza. Parking the bike I went closer and found the colonnade continued on all four sides of the square building. The warm golden colour of the stone contrasted with the grey walls behind. The structure had originally been the cloisters of a Carmelite monastery which, with the adjoining church, had been built over an eighty year period between 1726 and 1808. The inner court was paved with slate coloured tiles with dark red borders. The sweeping arches were repeated from one end to the other. Small market stalls lined the interior on one side with a convenient coffee counter near the escalators going down into the basement. I was not able to read the signs in either Spanish or Catalan but looking down I realized that there was an immense supermarket beneath the ancient cloisters. The escalators were ramped rather than stepped so as to accommodate loaded shopping carts. An ingenious design.

Mahon gives its name to mayonnaise or 'mahonesa.' Some say it was a sauce invented by the chef of the French commander besieging Mao in the 18th century; others that a local peasant woman served it as dressing on the salad of a French general involved in the siege. I saw an empty dark blue five litre tub labeled MAYONESA sitting outside the back of a restaurant so it must be popular on its home turf. The old central city is compacted into three large squares with Georgian mansions and classical Spanish apartments side by side. One can walk from one end of this old town to the other in less than ten minutes. The fish market has pinkish walls with massive white pillars enclosing a filigree wrought iron gateway. The roofs have red corrugated tiles; the inner buildings are tiled brick. I was impressed with the public buildings – a library, the museum of Minorca, a theatre and an ornate building housing the seat of government.

*We met an English Wesleyan parson on holiday from Barcelona and hailing us we stopped and had a talk with him.*

144

*He had been in Barcelona many years and could talk Spanish like a native. He was bitter against Roman Catholicism, and deplored the fact that the workers should carry them round on their backs but, no whisky being obtainable, I could not enter into a theological discussion with him especially as what we had really stopped for was to ask him to direct us to a decent cafe. He directed us to a club, largely used by Spanish officers and we had a most enjoyable tea, after which we had another walk round and a few drinks of Malaga wine, returning aboard highly satisfied with our afternoon's outing.*

Mao is built into the side of the cliff which flanks the port on the south shore. It is built on two levels. Along the harbour on the lower level is a low line of shops: ship's chandlers, cafes and restaurants. Here is the night life of Mao – clubs, music bars and neon lights. Up the road is a remnant of the British occupation – a gin factory. The guide book explained that the only local ingredient in the drink is Menorcan water for the junipers were killed off in a severe winter and no longer grow on the island. To reach the upper town the traveler either climbs a long set of steps or drives up a roadway consisting of successive hairpin bends built into the cliff. The pedestrian stairway leads up through a series of tiny parks where the traveller may rest weary legs. It is a 300 meter climb. On my last night I made my way down the steps to a restaurant I had discovered earlier in my stay. I had returned my rented bicycle that afternoon so it was a tough climb down and then back again after a full meal.

When I arrived in Mao I had taken a taxi from the airport because the bus service had closed for the night. But I

145

caught the bus for my return flight to Barcelona. The fare? €1.60 as compared with €27 for the taxi!

# CHAPTER 8: ALGIERS

My first impression of Algiers from the air was how green and lush the countryside looked. I was expecting it to be parched and brown, at the edge of the Sahara, but there were scores of small fields with neat rows of crops and fruit trees. Here and there was a modest house or a primitive-looking shack. By contrast, the airport was modern, all glass and concrete and convenient to negotiate. The official at Passport Control looked forbidding but after checking my passport through his scanner he welcomed me with a smile and said: "Canada – good country!" At the gate my man, whose name I later discovered was Mohammed, held up a sign with my name and "Tar Tlidjene Hotel." He had a walnut face with a cheery smile displaying his missing front teeth. His closely cropped silver beard and the way it was styled were evidence that he took care of his appearance. He wore a dark suit and a dark striped shirt which gave him the formal air befitting a driver. He quietly insisted on carrying my airline bag; I was immediately embarrassed, as a Canadian, by my lack of French when he asked in a soft voice whether I spoke either Arabic or French because he had no English. I followed him as he threaded his way deftly through crowds and traffic in the vast car park. Following him, I noticed that he walked with a limp, dragging one foot forward.

On our half-hour journey to the hotel I made some attempts at conversation in my fractured French: I commented on the number of speed bumps, telling him that in England these were called "gendarmes dormire" to which he replied "Oui, en Algiere 'sleeping police'." Touche! I was astonished at the number of police roadblocks we encountered: no sleeping policemen here, but watchful officers with fearsome-looking carbines and strange black boxes like portable radios with long antennae which they wafted over the cars. I later discovered that these were not walkie-talkies as I had guessed but "whiffie-sniffies" for detecting explosives. The guidebook stated that there had been bomb attacks around the country by dissidents two years before. Between the sleeping and the waking police the traffic was snarled up over and over again. However the autoroute sections were fast - very fast - with cars interweaving past each other well over the posted speed limit.

On arrival at the hotel I was warmly welcomed at the desk by the manager, Hamoudi, and his assistant, Maryam. I was treated to a tiny cup of espresso while they copied details from my passport. Tar Dlidgene Hotel (or 'Bording House' as the cards and paper napkins proclaimed) is in Ain Taya, a community about 30 kilometers from the centre of Algiers. The name means "house of friendship" - appropriately enough for I was offered dinner each night and driven to various places of interest at a very reasonable price. They made a point of serving Algerian specialties such as grilled fish and a delicious vegetable and meat soup called chorba. Breakfast was included with lodging. My room was large and the bathroom had gleaming blue and green Moorish tiles with mandala designs.

Algiers is now a city of 3.3 million. My grandfather thought the city a fair size in his day with a population of 154,000.

*We left Gibraltar on the afternoon of Wednesday the 8th and arrived at Algiers in Northern Africa on Friday where*

148

*we were to stay for a week. Algiers is the capital of Algeria and has a very extensive trade. A fair estimation of its size can be obtained from the fact that it has a population of over 154,000. The French quarter of Algiers has been called the second Paris but this statement must be taken with a grain of salt. It is not quite the City of Light that one expects to find after listening to the tales of former visitors. The shops are either of the tawdriest and most miserable aspect, or old curiosity bazaars, or flaring coffee houses or the fly traps of the Boulevards. These fly-traps, as in Paris, exhibit the identical wares that were exhibited in the time of Napoleon - the same picture frames and sham jewellery and licentious books and sealing-ware and note paper beloved of fops and chorus-girls.*

*There are some splendid public buildings the most notable of which are the Post Office, the Governor's Palace and the Citadel. There are two mosques in Algiers, the larger of which is called "El Kebir", and has an interesting history. Unfortunately the religious beliefs of its users bans the admission of Europeans within its sacred precincts.*

On my first morning I asked for a taxi to go to the centre of Algiers and search out the various places mentioned by grandfather. "No problem," said Hamoudi, "Mohammed and I will take you wherever you wish to go" So the three of us climbed into the nine-passenger van which had brought me from the airport the previous day. I had not noticed then that it was garishly painted red and yellow with the hotel name and "VERY CLEAN" emblazoned on it front and side. I sat behind them and Hamoudi would turn around from the front seat to describe a passing sight. He was a tall, burly man with a neatly trimmed moustache and thick expressive eyebrows. His English was good although he would sometimes fumble for a word and consult with Mohammed in Arabic. He was dressed in a tailored grey-flannel suit with a cashmere sweater under the jacket and dress shoes which eventually got saturated with the steady rain as we walked around. His clothes gave him a distinctly English look. He told me that he was new to the hotel business as he had been a career officer in the army.

The population of Algiers has more than doubled in the past 20 years, evidence of which we saw as we drove through the sprawling suburbs where old apartments, small shops and newer industrial buildings crowded the busy streets. As we neared the city centre, the mean streets were replaced by wide boulevards with whitewashed buildings dating back to the French era. The 5-storey colonnaded buildings along the seafront with bright blue railings reminded me strongly of the seafront in Nice. Probably they date from about the same time too. I soon discovered that much of downtown Algiers situated below the Casbah and the Citadel was laid out as the "Ville Nouvelle" after the visit of the Emperor Napoleon III and his Empress, Eugenie, in 1860. The tawdry shops and coffee houses described by grandfather were not in evidence in this rebuilt area abutting the ocean.

Our first objective was the Old Port where grandfather had landed. The rain fell steadily and a cold wind buffeted the shore. This was December, the wettest month of the year in Algiers. The harbour, with its old buildings, was well protected by two breakwaters from the wild Mediterranean seas outside. My van Gogh styled umbrella offered me little protection and it took an effort to keep it from being blown inside out. One set of buildings topped by a tower resembling a lighthouse was the administrative headquarters of the Algerian Navy. It would have been there in grandfather's time, according to Hamoudi. The harbour itself contained a few small runabouts with outboard motors--the bigger ships were in the newer section of the busy port or in the roadsteads outside. Algiers is the busiest port in northwest Africa. Imports include raw materials and industrial products while exports consist of oil, phosphates, iron ore, oranges and other agricultural items. The city is known colloquially as 'Alger la Blanche' for its white, glistening buildings rising up from the sea.

*The harbour is exceptionally busy, not altogether on account of its large trade but because it is used as a coaling port by many of the merchant vessels trading in the Mediterranean and beyond it. It is within easy reach of Gibraltar, Marseilles and Malta and has many visitors of the globe trotting type, notably Americans. There was a Yankee millionaire visiting the port while we were there and, by lavish display and ostentation, managed to create a bit of a sensation. I can't stand the Yankee at any price, especially the patronizing sort with their flap-doodle, Mr. Roosevelt, the statue of Liberty, the Chicago meat trade, the Tammany bosses, the almighty dollar, the New York policeman, the gin-sling, the state of the weather, George Washington, and Doctor Cook of the North Pole and so on ad nauseam.*

Before visiting the other sites grandfather describes, Hamoudi asked me to look up to the western edge of the city. Algiers rises up from a huge crescent-shaped bay; the glistening white building he showed me was at the top of a hill at the western horn of the crescent.

"Have you heard about the church we call Madame Afrique?" he said.

"Tell me about it" I replied, in order to hear a description from him.

"That is our name for it; it is actually the Notre Dame d'Afrique and it has recently been restored. If you like, Shayms, I can show you."

"Yes, I would like to see it – my grandfather didn't write about it."

"Well he should have because it was built long ago by the French White Fathers. It was here when he was."

"Perhaps it was weather like this and he did not look up through the rain," I replied.

"We go" he said.

It was a hair-raising trip – steep, winding streets with very little room for two cars to pass and frequent hair pin bends. It was a relief when we parked in the wide cobbled churchyard and emerged from the van. My discomfort was worth the visit; the unusual Byzantine-styled church was built by French colons in 1872. The site is on a 120-meter-high plateau overlooking the busy city where two French ladies from Lyon had placed a statue of the virgin to help them remember the shrine above their home city. It got its name from the statue of the Black Madonna above the altar. Around the edge of the yard sheep were grazing, oblivious of the city far beneath or the shining sacred building behind them. For me they were a reminder of the rural origins of the vast capital. The name of the Djemaa Ketchaoua mosque in the heart of the old town or Casbah means "place of the goats." That is where we drove to next, down the winding lane of donkey carts and near misses.

Grandfather mentions seeing three public buildings and two mosques during his stay in Algiers but says little about them. Djemaa Ketchaoua dates back to the 17th century. Remodelled in 1794 by the ruler of Algiers, Hassan Pasha, when he built his palace adjoining it, a plaque tells us that the French placed a cross on the top and renamed it the Cathedral of St Philippe. So it was a Roman Catholic church in grandfather's time; I guess he failed to look up and see the cross. It was decorated by French artists, visited by Napoleon III and the organ was played by Saint-Saens in 1873. Two days after Algeria regained independence in 1862 it was reconsecrated as a mosque. Unfortunately both the mosque and the palace next door were under renovation so I could not enter them. The palace was given a new façade with rows of windows and balconies by the French occupiers. It became, as grandfather says, the governor's residence. Apparently much of the interior decoration - in the form of wall tiles, ornate plasterwork and painted ceilings - has survived.

Djemaa el-Kebir (or Great Mosque) is down towards the port and also has a mixed pedigree. Both Berbers and Phoenicians built a place of worship on this site which the Romans later converted into a temple. Then it became a Christian basilica before finally being replaced by a mosque in the 11th century, which makes it the oldest in the city. The inscription on the minaret urges viewers to contemplate its beauty. I did. The facade along the treed avenue consists of a

153

long row of Moorish arches of white marble and crenellated like the buildings in the Alhambra in Granada. Above them is a row of blue tiles, then a second row of crenellated white tiles across the roof line. The blue tiled minaret with its white dome rises high over the south-west corner and contrasts with the backdrop of white buildings and the blue ocean beyond. Inside the ornate entrance, which is flanked by an additional set of columns and arches, is a further series of white Moorish arches forming the worship area. The floor tiles are cream with an etched pattern of white arches echoing those above. The inner walls are again covered with blue tiles decorated with filigreed gold Arabic texts. I viewed the outside once more across a shining, rain-swept square in front of yet another mosque, the Djemaa-el-Djedid or New Mosque. Legend has it, I was told, that the architect of this mosque was a Christian and designed it in the form of a Greek cross; when his trickery was uncovered he was executed.

Who would imagine that a Post Office would be one of the must-see sites in a city? Yet grandfather did see it and so did I. It is a Moorish-style building dating from 1908 so it would have been newly completed in his time. It stands at the intersection of two converging streets, a hexagonal structure with a set of steps leading up to three huge portals three storeys high. Blue glazed tiles curve around the doorways with a blue and gold sign in Arabic above. The proportions of the whole structure with its arched windows had me in awe just as I felt years before at the Alhambra. It looks more like a palace than a post office.

One hundred and eighty meters above the city and its port the Citadel stands guard. The original structure dates back to early Berber times; the present massive fortification was built by the brother of the famed pirate turned statesman,

Barbarossa – he of the Red Beard. Like many notable historic buildings in Algiers, the Citadel was closed for renovations. But the view from its high walls was stunning. Contained within the walls are a palace with quarters for a harem and a mosque in addition to the barracks. In 1816, the ruler of Algiers, Dey Ali, moved there from his palace near the harbour during a bombardment of the city by the British. It took 76 mules to move his gold and silver treasures with him. This was the third of the three public buildings which so impressed my grandfather. They are mentioned only in passing, for his main focus was on the area known as the Casbah, the district surrounding the fortress.

Once we had found parking nearby, the three of us walked into the narrow laneways of the ancient Casbah. Led by Hamoudi we stepped from the bustle of commerce into a hushed world. We clambered up steep cobbled pavements with stairways and encountered no cars. At times the experience reminded me of walking in an old growth forest, for some of the houses leaned towards each other overhead while some had huge beams across the alleyways to prevent them falling into one another. Some were ramshackle, some semi-demolished; although there has been massive rebuilding by the government to provide more housing. The whole area has been listed by UNESCO as a World Heritage site and described as 'one of the finest coastal cities in the Mediterranean'. At several points during our wander, Hamoudi stopped to ask the way. I was not sure where he was aiming to take us; perhaps he was seeking the way out. In any event I found it a fascinating tour with magnificent views over the city. In the 1937 film "Pepe le Moko" (and in the later remake "Algiers" with Charles Boyer) the main character knows that he is safe from the police so long as he stays within its confines because they dared not venture in. The

155

labyrinthine laneways of dwellings, shops and mosques provided a clandestine haven for the F.L.N. (National Liberation Front) during the planning and launching of attacks against the French forces during their struggle for independence. One and a half million Algerians lost their lives during the conflict so vividly portrayed in Pontecorvo's film, *The Battle of Algiers*. There is now a police presence in the Casbah but travellers are still warned not to visit certain areas, particularly after dark, just as grandfather was. He and his companions went anyway.

*Arab town Algiers is well worth a visit but if possible it should be explored in daylight as the Arabs do not respect the same moral code as we do and it isn't a heinous offence in their eyes to stick a knife in a European and relieve him of his money and jewellery. I had Hobson's choice and had to go through this quarter late in the evening. Fortunately I got two companions and acting on the old adage that there is safety in numbers we hung together and dived into one of the dingy streets that led into the centre of Arab town. The houses are built very close together and in some cases, where signs of decay had set in, the walls on either side had inclined inwards and actually touched at the top. It was not the houses however we had come to see but their inhabitants and this was rendered easy by the fact that there are no doors and windows to restrict the view and one can see the inmates squatting over their evening meal or nonchalantly puffing at a cigarette and seemingly indifferent to the outside world. There are many small shops in this quarter and the dusky keepers sit outside and praise the quality of their goods. Now and again we had to flatten ourselves against the walls to let some great hulking Arab Sheik pass, as we were ignorant of the rules of the road and thought it good policy to show these Arabs that we were at least civil and inoffensive. The Arab and the Bedouin are really desert dwellers and in their natural wandering life are quite moral and peaceable but when herded in a town, especially a seaport town, wickedness and vice breaks out and flourishes like the proverbial bay tree.*

After our walk through the Casbah we drove to the Jardin d'Essai, a vast public park which Hamoudi wanted me to see. As we got out of the car it started to hail – not for long, fortunately. We had a wet, misty walk through avenues of rare trees past little lagoons with bedraggled waterfowl peering disconsolately at us. The hail had let up after a brief rattle. Beyond the gardens we glimpsed a huge concrete monument consisting of three intertwined palm fronds. According to Hamoudi they symbolized the unity of Algeria's three strands: culture, industry and agriculture. It is 92m in height and was financed by the Canadian engineering company SNC-Lavalin. It is dedicated to the Unknown Martyr who died for his country in the war of independence.

That evening I was invited to join in the celebrations for a wedding that was to take place in the hotel the following Saturday. This feast was the first of the traditional three days leading up to the wedding and was for male guests only. We sat down to a lavish meal during which I was introduced to the groom. He was a young man in his thirties who spoke perfect English, which was not surprising, for he was a pilot with Delta Airlines. I was made welcome among the group of Arabic-speaking strangers. Unlike North American stag parties there were no pornographic movies and no alcohol. There were so many guests that we ate in relays. As we left we

157

were each given a decorative box of sweetmeats. The following evening it was the ladies night and they whooped it up with loud music and dancing. How different from grandfather's entertainment:


*I went to some of the drink shops and was robbed right and left. I had the option to go inside and sit on gold plush seats in a stifling atmosphere of petroleum and patchouli or sit shivering at a hard round table in the street exposed to the insults of curio sellers and the importunities of professional beggars. As we walked on we passed dozens of houses where you could hire a woman's body from a 2 franc piece upwards. I said woman's body but many of them have not reached womanhood and appeared to be mere girls and no doubt are procured from the country districts and are nothing more nor less than slaves to some old sheik who kneels down in the great mosque and thanks Mohammed that he is not as other men are. These girls are decked out in all the glitter and tinsel that belong to the calling and look very inviting in the artificial light.*

*Not being better than any of my fellow mortals, I am*

*not going to sit in judgement upon them and their trade but prefer to leave the matter to the common sense of the visitor whether he buys what they offer for hire or spends his francs in some other way for did not the great Christ himself stoop to raise Magdalene from the dust and show compassion for her and who knows might have shown her something else besides. The French quarter is just as bad and in the cafes and in the streets one gets the stare and the wink which proclaims to the world the harlots trade and which if followed up ends usually in clinching a bargain already half made. I have nothing to do*

158

*with other people's business and I am neither upholding nor condemning prostitution as I fancy the extremists on both sides are wrong. Nature has some very rigid laws regarding sexual relations and as we are governed by natures' laws' nature will exact a heavy penalty if we abuse the trust she has reposed in us as far as propagating our species is concerned. Prostitution is as old as history itself, has been banned by the churches and the "Unco guid" for centuries, but has a firmer root today amongst the nations than Christianity itself.*

The following day Mohammed and I set off once more in the 9 passenger bus for a trip into Algeria's Roman past. This time another Mohammed sat alongside him. The freeway took us most of the way along the coast. The prosperous looking countryside was dotted with fertile farms and plush resorts. Then, 60 kilometers west of Algiers we arrived at Tipaza, a dusty village which fronts the ruins of a Roman town complex on the seafront. There is a theatre, an arena and a temple interspersed among the foundations of numbers of houses. In one there was a complete floor of mosaic tiles on which Mohammed the younger jumped repeatedly to sound out the hollow basement beneath. I was shocked to see visitors being allowed to climb all over the ancient walls. Don't the authorities know the damage inflicted on Stonehenge by clambering visitors? Some of the larger houses had channels in the floors – I presume for central heating. The setting on the foreshore with the main artery extending almost into the waves brought stone, ocean and sky blues together.

We then drove to more Roman ruins in a nearby village named Cherchell. They are not as well preserved as in Tipaza, partly because they are situated in the midst of various back streets and roads. The town has grown over the ruins. The most illuminating part of our visit was seeing beautiful Roman mosaics and a collection of pottery all gathered at the site. On our way home we drove up into the hills to explore an ancient mausoleum. Shaped like a massive beehive with rough stone blocks fronted by a beautiful palisade of Doric style columns it has recently been carbon dated to the $5^{th}$ Century BC or before. For many years it was thought to date back to the $1^{st}$ Century BC, in the time of the Numidian kings, perhaps constructed for a royal occupant. But its origins are shrouded in mystery.

On the day of my departure from Algeria, after being dropped off at the airport by the ever-faithful Mohammed, I discovered that leaving Algiers was far more complicated than arriving. For a start there was a complete security check complete with metal detection at the entrance to the airport building. Between the ticket counter and the door into the aircraft itself, there were no less than three further checkpoints including a final pat down on the corridor to the plane. Delays and line-ups made the process tedious. However my fascinating five-day stay made it all worthwhile. Algeria was the final stop on my journey through the Mediterranean with my grandfather's diary as my guide.

# CHAPTER 9: A LIFE ON THE OCEAN WAVE

This chapter brings together the personal strands in my grandfather's narrative, namely: his enforced recruitment in the Royal Navy, his ridicule of naval customs, and his radical political beliefs. At the beginning of the project my aim was to travel to the places in the Mediterranean he describes in his diary, and write about my own observations and thoughts one hundred years later while integrating the two accounts. His skills of observation and his facility with words in his lucid accounts of places and people I have found remarkable, especially since he did not have much formal education. His unfailing curiosity and the way he addresses an audience adds mystery to his character. The broader theme which emerged as I traveled was my delight in getting to know a man who died 23 years before I was born. He spoke most clearly to me in his opinions about the navy and in his attitudes to capitalism and to the sufferings of the poor in Britain and in the countries he saw. He had an informed grasp on economics and politics; much of which is still relevant to the chaotic conditions we live in today.

Here's how he describes his reactions on seeing a company of British soldiers marching past him in Gibraltar:

*It was a change to be away from England right away from Chatham and to feast ones eyes on houses and costumes that were not all drab or black and white. Here was a wealth of green and red, and strong, blazing yellow, and purple, rich and proud. And then a company of English Tommies passed to the music of a band, in their khaki uniforms and big, queer peaked caps, with their honest, ugly English faces grinning under them. The English type of face was there, or, shall I say, one of the English types. And it was good to see.*

*In a moment there came to us a vision of the empire. From east to west, in half a dozen British stations, burnt by uncongenial and relentless suns, battered by cold rain or stung by icy winds, those lean, brown English faces, as English as the Mile End Road or Nottingham market, or star fair, or the sixpenny side at old Trafford, were grinning their saucy, good humored, cynical English grin. One's heart warmed to Tommy, one remembered their hardships in South Africa, fighting in the interest of the Berthsteins and De Beers who wanted cheap labour for their mines, their weary marches and muddy camps. And the drums and fifes were playing - who does not know the thrill of the drums and fifes? There on the foreign rock, in the street of the foreign town, the English fifes and drums were playing an English quickstep as old as Waterloo, possibly as old as Bannockburn or Flodden, and back went our spirits with a bound to Southsea Common and Chatham lines. When the drums throb and rattle and the fifes squeal the blood changes its pace and the colour of the world is not the same. The call of the fife and drum is a real call; a call imperative.*

*The song they sing, no matter what the tune, is a song like that of the Sirens. The call of the fifes and drums is like the call of the sea. It is a summons to march, a summons to dare. It draws the prosaic, unimaginative merry English lad out of his sleepy village, out of the turmoil of the strident town. It draws him under the spell of the barracks and the discipline; it transforms him into a Tommy; it draws him after it across the seven seas, to the desert, or the mountains, or the heat blistered plains. It draws him into hardship, into*

162

*sickness, into danger, into suffering; it keeps him strenuous, it keeps him daring, it keeps him cheerful, and it marches him to the homeward-bound troopship, and marches him through the streets of Southampton, or Portsmouth, or Queenstown and past the barrack gates and the guard-room, so that his journeys and adventures, his wounds and fatigues and all the strange faces and places he has seen become to him as a dream.*

*But ever from the day when the spell is first laid upon him the call of the fife and drum is in his blood, and in his bones, and in the grey matter of his brain; and when he hears the weird song, be it that his eyes are dim and his hair grey, be the song sung to him in a city street amid the brawl of the tide of traffic, or let him hear it on the Rock of Gibraltar or in an English village lane, his heart shall be young again. He shall hold up his head, and the drab world shall glow with colour and the things that to the market men seem wild impossibilities shall be once more to him, the man who has seen and done them, the only real things in life. And yet the song of the fife is not a merry song. The thrill of it is a cold thrill. The core of the music is plaintive. The notes which lure men into high endeavour, into reckless daring, into mad adventure are notes not far from tears.*

I have read and reread this passage. It's beautiful, it's poetic, and it's informed. The fife and drum calls the soldier to acts of courage and endurance, or arouses an old veteran from the drudgery of his civilian life into colourful memories of life in the British army.

Poignancy turns to humor, when he mocks the pointless and sometimes absurd naval routines:

163

## SHIPS ROUNDS

*The rounds of a ship on a Sunday morning are a very edifying spectacle. A water carnival is held on Saturday in preparation for the ordeal. Chaos reigns supreme on Sunday morning and such mundane things as breakfast or an extra hour in bed are taboo. Brooms and bucket and bucket and brooms are flourished in your face or tickle your ribs from early morning until about nine o'clock when, after boatswains mates have blown their calls and shouted themselves hoarse, a mass of humanity struggle into pursers rigs and sort themselves out on deck.*

*The cooks and sweepers remain behind to hide away anything that might offend the eagle eye of the Captain and train. The rounds start at 9-30, the Captain leading the way and about fifty following behind. There is, however, very little originality displayed among Naval Captains and I often wonder the whole thing doesn't strike them as a screaming farce, but I am afraid they are removed so far above the common herd that they have shed their sense of humour. Be this as it may they all say pretty much the same thing when going the rounds of a ship or divisions of men. They all have a howl about seamen's bags. Bag tallies must be clean, numbers up and inboard. What an effort! Stokers and Engine Room Artificers' baths not clean. Perdition. Mess shelves look as if recently used. Good God! A pair of boots stowed overhead. At this juncture a cold sweat breaks out on the brow of the No. 1 and the assembled mob looks guiltily from one to another and mutter about the empire being in imminent peril and the tension is only relieved by the jaunty* (master-at-arms) *rushing up and taking the name of the criminal.*

164

*The retinue then adjourn to the upper deck where a lot of lay figures, dubbed men so as to prevent them being in any way confused with officers, are decked out in a uniform designed by some crank at the Admiralty and set up to a plank seam waiting for inspection. The routine here is to tell every third or fourth man that he wants a hair-cut or shave or that some seam does not conform to the regulations by about a thousandth part of an inch and a reputation for zeal can always be earned by carrying an ivory rule in the pocket. This part of the comedy over, true to the Christian traditions of the British Navy, church is rigged and another act in the comedy is entered upon. When the curtain is finally rung down, rum is served out and things gradually assume their normal condition and the articles that have been placed behind the scenes are brought out until the day for the next rehearsal.*

## AN INSPECTION BY THE REAR ADMIRAL

*We had come under the command of a new Rear Admiral and a little excitement prevailed when a signal was received that he would inspect us on Sunday. There was the usual preparation for his reception, only on a greater scale than usual. The ship was rubbed over from stem to stern with paint and the brightwork got an unusual burnishing up and the ships' company practised walking in space for a week previous. At muster by the open list I recognised the gentleman who had caused all the commotion to be a former Captain of mine and figures in my book already as the man who said "If we hadn't been in the Navy we should have been in the workhouse or probably in prison". He was slung out of the Navy never to have another command again for allowing a ragging case to take place aboard his ship but the great*

165

*British Public soon forgot and he managed to worm himself back again remembering no doubt his own philosphy about the <u>workhouse</u> and <u>prison</u>. He spent two years organising the Turkish Navy which was a job under British government and has learned his work well as an Admiral. He can tell to a nicety if a Cap badge is central or has worked round to the right or left. He can smell a man who wants a haircut twenty yards away and his powers of complimentary language regarding dickie tapes or silk knots or pussers boots awed even our experienced Captain.*

## AN EXERCISE ASHORE

*On the morning of August 29^th we were startled by the unusual pipe of "Land every available man". I looked round and saw everyone beginning to get into everyone else's way which is not a very difficult job on a man of war, owing to the lack of space each man is allowed. To make matters more cheerful, we had started painting the day previous, so that our gear was anywhere except where it should have been. The marines made a gallant charge on their storeroom - a place in which it would be impossible to swing the proverbial cat - and found their rifles all in a heap. I don't think they stopped to sort them out, but acted up to the well known "Navyism" "It runs one each". The seamen didn't fare much better: the majority found their implements of war stored in the copper dams and they also made use of the above mentioned "navyism".*

*During this time our fellow sufferers, the stokers, had emerged from the nether regions to get out the boats in which we were to land; after which they had to get ready themselves. After getting ourselves sorted out and rigged, we endeavoured*

166

*to fill our water bottles as the orders were "filled water bottles." The tanks were dry but, as we hadn't had any breakfast, what did it matter about a little water? Our next move was to get into the boat, which had been prepared for us. Someone in authority - I could tell he was an officer by the ridiculous public school accent - ordered us to fill our water bottles with salt water while we were being taken ashore. I didn't obey the order, neither did I see anyone else do so and, I expect, had it been real instead of acting, we should all have been shot. What a glorious commencement of an engagement, yeomen shot for refusing to obey the order of a madman, for who but a man bereft of his senses would think of giving such a command?*

*We landed at Valetta and marched to Florian Parade in a cross between a quick and a double march. A place was allotted to us in which to form up, which we did, only to find it was the wrong place. We had to repeat this several times before we found ourselves on the spot intended for us. We then had to await the remainder of the fleet. I took advantage of this brief spell to have a look round. I saw sailors or stokers - I couldn't discern which - standing about at various intervals to represent posts (we are very useful at times) while further away and occupying the great position was his most divine Kingship the Admiral surrounded by his staff. I wondered if he had salt water for his breakfast. I didn't have too much time for meditation as the other ships' companies began to arrive and we had to fall in. Some ships' companies marched on in style; they had their bands playing but even the music failed to cheer the faces of the "men." (I didn't have time to observe the officers' countenances). As I stood and dreamed I thought of Jack's happy smile, the sprightly step and rolling gait that he is supposed to have.*

167

*The Navy is supposed to be a model of uniformity and it ought to be, considering the money and time that is spent in trying to make it so. Yet there were some companies with jumpers on, some with none, others had leggings on, others didn't and some had coats while others thought the weather too warm to carry such a heavy article of apparel. We next formed up for a ceremonial review - if such a thing can be imagined under the circumstances. Personally I have no clear conception as to what we really did. I simply followed the mob as did the remainder. I remember marching round several times just narrowly missing the posts - I mean the men who were representing posts - to the tune of "A life on the ocean wave" and "Nancy Lee," after which we tried to form up in line and advance in review order. This was so bad that we had to repeat it. What can one expect on a diet of salt water? I don't think his sereneness was very well pleased with our attempt. Judging from the way he sent us back to our ships I should say he allowed his liver to get the better of him for he ordered us to double back to the landing stage. That double back: I don't think I shall ever forget it. Everyone was running down hill, some shouting, some cursing and swearing, others laughing and making a joke of it. Companies got mixed up, sailors in marines companies and stokers mixed with seaman. Cruisers ships companies mixed with destroyers detachments and ambulance parties got so much mixed with the ammunition bearers that you couldn't tell "t'other from which". According to drill books, armies in retreat should retire in an orderly manner so as not to encourage the enemy. I don't know what an enemy would have thought had they seen us scramble down Calcara Hill. I suppose it was the Great One's idea of naval discipline. We returned aboard about 9-20 a.m. with no one hurt; a fitting conclusion to such a farcical absurdity.*

In his rant about the navy's obsession with spit, polish and brasswork, his humour turns sardonic, almost Monty Pythonesque, as when he suggests that a special cleaning ship be towed behind the warships. I found myself cheering at this. At high school we were required to join either the Naval Cadets or the Army Corps. I joined the Sea Cadets because I liked the sea and ships. I was often criticized by the lieutenant in charge for my slovenly appearance on the parade ground; my uniform was not properly creased or my shoes were not shined. I was there to learn about knots and rigging, compass reading, charts and sailing a whaler. Marching and drills were of no interest. The high point for me was a 3-day voyage on a South African Navy minesweeper between Port Elizabeth and Durban, where the annual two week summer camp was held.

## NAVAL HIERARCHY

*People will persist in telling you that Jack and his officers being thrown so much together on board ship become rare helpmates to one another, and this tends to level down the class barrier. Splendid pictures of "coal ship" are shown by our press, representing officers and men sharing the toil and the man in the street smiles and says to himself, "How friendly, what good friends they are". Well, well, I hope he carries on thinking so as it is a well known fact that he British public are in woeful ignorance as regards the inner workings and relations between Jack and his officers.*

*Everyone I think knows that the Navy is officered by the sons of our middle and upper classes and this has been going on so long that people look upon it as a perfectly natural sequence. One must admit however that money cannot purchase brains and the wealthy classes have no monopoly of* brain power. One day in this democratic age Jack might begin to inquire why he has not even a sporting chance to attain to the higher positions in his calling but is doomed to be a mere automaton, a unit to the end of his days though by a little development he might have been a Togo or a second Nelson.

The existing officers are not wholly opposed to a scheme which would ensure a greater number of promotions from the lower deck. In fact, in the issue of the Naval and Military Record of December 14th, 1910 there was outlined a scheme of promotion, submitted by an executive officer, in which almost every detail was provided for to ensure the success of the proposed innovation. What, however, is worth more than passing notice is that such a democratic revolution should have for its sponsors officers holding executive rank in the Royal Navy, when it is considered that the Wardroom doorway is the most difficult of all the doorways in British bureaucratic life to enter, not excepting Parliament itself. The enemies of the scheme have fought it on the ground that there would be a lack of refinement in the new type of officer. Ye gods! Refinement! Fifty per cent of refinement consists of hot water, soap, clothes, and a clean tablecloth. Like the girl in "Punch", who preferred being pretty to being good, because she could always be good when she wanted to, I would prefer a man to be zealous and intelligent and trust to him attaining a certain degree of culture when he wanted it. A man's messmates will excuse lack of refinement in a keen and able officer. But a turret or an engine room will not excuse a highly refined officer for not knowing how to load and fire its guns or how to work and repair the engines. In the rush and stress of war and of daily work in the fleet, culture counts but for very little. There is a lot of truth in the saying that home spun stands more wear and tear than lace. This however is by the way.

He observed other instances where special treatment was given to officers compared to that meted out to those "below deck."

*We entered the harbour of Palermo on the morning of Wednesday the 21st and, as we had been eagerly looking forward to our visit here, we were on deck early to have the first glimpse of the place we had heard so much about. We of the lower deck got rather a rude shock when we were coolly informed that no leave would be granted during our stay as there was an epidemic of fever in the town. This did not deter the officers from going ashore and when, on the following day, several townspeople came to visit the ship and sell postcards to the officers, I made it my business to find out to what extent the fever was raging in the town. As I shrewdly guessed, there was absolutely no reason why the men should be kept aboard; on good authority I was told that there were only two cases of fever and that the patients were isolated outside the town. The health of Palermo as a whole was excellent. There was something behind this shady business because if, in the opinion of the Admiral, the fever was so prevalent that it might be carried to the ships, then it was criminal on his part to allow officers to freely come and go about the town and mix with the ship's companies, thus risking the lives of nearly two thousand souls.*

*The evening before our departure was made the occasion for a grand reception and ball given by the Admiral and officers of our squadron to the elite of Algiers. Two ships, the Lancaster and Suffolk, were hauled close together and connected by a broad carpeted gangway. This arrangement provided for plenty of space for dancing and also for refreshment and supper tables. We of the lower deck were carefully shut out from this act by means of the ships' bunting and rolls of canvas and in consequence could only catch a glimpse of some fair charmer in evening dress or our officers in their elegant trappings through a chink in the temporary walls.*

*We discharged the ratings in Chatham that had taken passage and some tons of officers' baggage was landed and dispatched to its various destinations. Though Jack's bundle is subjected to a thorough search by the dockyard police in case he is trying to land some government stores; the officers' packages are passed on their word of honor (?) But I who am writing with an inside knowledge know that this method is adopted to prevent widespread scandal.*

My first taste of the prejudice permeating the English class system came when I arrived in London from South Africa at the age of 25 to do graduate work in psychology on a British Council scholarship. To make scholars feel at home the Council arranged for us to meet local families. I was invited for dinner by Sir Benjamin Huggett and his wife and their two daughters who were in their twenties. During conversation over sherry before dinner it became clear to me that Sir Benjamin was unable to identify my social status from my South African accent so he asked some probing questions including what my father did for a living. University professor appeared to pass the test for I was subsequently allowed to take his daughter out on a date. She told me about her father's doubts; he expected her to be particularly careful around "the colonial" as he referred to me. None of this had been apparent when he welcomed me at his substantial front door.

The subtle way in which the English assess one's social class was a contrast to the open racism I had become accustomed to in South Africa and yet the prejudice and discrimination underlying both racism and classism were similar. The subtlety in England reminded me of a black friend telling me that he preferred the direct racist expressions of the Afrikaans whites to the subtle ways of the English- speaking South Africans. "At least I know exactly where I stand with a Boer," he said.

Numerous similar experiences of class prejudice were part of my family's decision to immigrate to Canada after seven years in England. Grandfather might be surprised that the system he resented still holds sway all these years later.

## GRIPES ABOUT THE NAVY

Hours of work

*There is a book kept by the Engineer and signed by the Captain every week and in this book the Engine Room Artificers were duly credited with 40 ½ hours a week at their respective trades. Not much to grumble at there; this compares very favourably with trade union hours. It looks grand on paper, but in reality 60 to 80 hours a week is much nearer the mark on many of our ships and, if anyone in this branch cared to keep a careful record of the hours worked daily during a commission, it would take the starch out of that splendid song, the chorus of which says "Britons never, never shall be slaves".. Emphasis on the two nevers please.*

Army versus Navy

*On my second visit ashore in Malta I found my way to the Sergeants' mess of the Argyle and Sutherland Highlanders and met many old friends whom I had known when the regiment was stationed in Chatham. It is delightful to sit in a comfortable arm chair on a shady verandah with a few sergeants, each with a long cool glass of beer, leaning back among their cushions and talking about being overworked. I once heard a prominent politician say that the life of a sergeant in a Highland Regiment was quite up to the standard of an ordinary M.P. There is a great deal of truth in this statement as there is no doubt that they are treated in quite a different manner from their corresponding ranks in the Navy. They are comfortably messed, have billiard, reading and smoking rooms and a bar where liquors of the finest quality are supplied at the lowest possible cost. Apart from their material wants being well catered for they enjoy to a man the confidence and esteem of their superior officers.*

*In the Navy a Chief Petty Officer, notwithstanding the fact that he is the senior rating on the lower deck, is allowed practically no more privileges than the most junior rating carried. He is only allowed in his mess at certain times and in no way can he look upon it as a home. The Captain, commander or even some junior officer is always poking his nose inside and finding fault if everything is not as prison-like as Naval Custom can make it. He is not allowed to smoke in his mess; neither can he have refreshment there. And twice a week the Captain has a look in the locker in which the C.P.O.'s private gear is stowed and if everything is not nicely laid out on top then as likely as not a turn of leave stopped is the result. The Engine.Room .Artificers come in for special attention as they have a locker provided in their bath for stowing greasy clothing. The first commandment in the Naval catechism says "there shall be no dirty overalls stowed in an E.R.A.'s locker", though where they should be stowed I have never heard from the autocrats who interpret these commandments.*

Christmas on board

*Xmas day landed on a Sunday and was observed in the usual Naval fashion. I need not enlarge upon how a ship is decorated or in what way Xmas is observed as anyone who has been to a workhouse at home can from a good idea of how things are carried out in the Navy. Hands are called at 5-30 a.m and the morning is spent in the usual way, namely scrubbing decks and polishing brightwork, until breakfast is piped. Division and Divine Service are attended as usual and as a fair testimony, as to how happy a time can be had aboard ship on Xmas day, can be gathered from the fact that everyone who has any money and not required for duty, push off ashore as soon as leave is granted. A few enthusiasts deck out the messes with colored papers and bits of green twigs and by piling a few oranges on a pusser's plate a fair imitation of an English Xmas is obtained. In my opinion a much better way would be to let the ship's company spend the day in whatever way they pleased. I mean, if they preferred to spend it in their hammock they would be at perfect liberty to do so, in short give them one day in the year on which they owned no master and could call the ship their home. This seems an awful proposition to make, but I do not think the consequences would be serious, because if you think of it there are times when men are free from discipline and away from all routine, yet their behaviour is not such as to warrant curtailing in any way their freedom to do just exactly as they pleased. However, our Xmas came and went and as we sailors are always*

175

*wishing our allotted spans away nothing remained now but to wish for the next one to come round quick, not because Xmas makes much difference one way or another, but they are milestones on the road to the end of a commission.*

Incompetence of Engineers

*In books of fiction the Engineers are pictured as brave fearless men with long square jaws and nerves of steel but I am sorry to say the Navy types are a sorry lot. They are generally nervous wrecks and the courage they possess is generally of the Dutch order and, when anything happens in the way of a breakdown, they stand with gloves on like the fabled cat which couldn't catch mice and shout at the E.R.A.'s and stokers who do the actual work. They receive a very expensive training that is mostly theoretical, and some ships carry as many as seven or eight. I am well within the mark in saying that they never touch a tool and, even if you defend them from the specialist point of view, they are sadly lacking, as they are prompted in nearly all cases by us working engineers, namely the E.R.A.'s. A good clerk could do all the book work in the department and one engineer well up in organising powers could supervise the department and do all that was necessary. A man-of-war is the last place where there is room for a kid glove type. There are many defects that develop on a modern ship in a short space of time and everyone with any pretense to being called an engineer should bear a hand even if it was only to do some useful work such as clearing a bilge suction or carrying water to the men who are at work.*

*The E.R.A.'s and stokers may have permission from the Engineer to go ashore, but, as a non-executive officer, he has practically no command over the department he is supposed to rule. He may give a make and mend to his department but unless it coincides with the upper deck one his men have to hide themselves away. They may be quite eligible to go ashore on that afternoon but are stopped because the sailors are at work. However on the Lancaster make and mends did not worry us much as we usually spent them down below toying with crankheads or hunting after leaks until the majority of us felt C.B.F. (Chock-block-full) or, in Naval parlance, W.W. There is much talk about engineering in the Navy being the most important branch of the service but it will always be subservient to the fads and customs of the old Nelsonian days unless the new class of officer, who is per programme to be as efficient in the engine room as on the bridge, sweeps away the hoary traditions and ancient customs which are ridiculous on a modern fighting ship.*

Despite his criticisms, he does show some understanding of the engineers' powerlessness compared with other officers in the ship's chain of command. And he does admire one engineer for an act of generosity:

*On Friday the 9<sup>th</sup> of September we steamed alongside the old mole and painted ship in readiness for coaling and steam trial. The crew by this time were settling down and working better together and a coal ship in quick time was effected on the Monday. Wednesday morning found us lit up all round and at eight o'clock we crept slowly outside the breakwater and started working up to full speed. The trial lasted twenty four hours and at nine o'clock the following morning we dropped anchor at Port Mahon in Minorca. The trial proved very successful, in fact so much so that the senior*

177

*engineer sent a bottle of whisky along to our mess, which tangible token of esteem was received by my messmates with mixed feelings of suspicion and awe. Personally, I took my share without experiencing any conscientious qualms and with true Scottish blood in my veins hoped that the engineer might contract a habit of sending along a bottle every night.*

## PERSONAL REACTIONS AND REVELATIONS

A War Game

*We were now under typical war conditions as very little food was obtainable and anyone in the Engineers department who could boast of four hours sleep out of the twenty four was looked upon as an extremely lucky individual. The guns were cleared away ready for action and the upper deck branch put in a good many hours standing by them. Personally, I don't like playing at war and sincerely hope I am a thousand leagues away when anything of a real nature comes along. I am not at all bloodthirsty and bear no grudge against my fellow workers, no matter what their colour or nationality, but being a hired assassin I must be an accessory whether I like it or not.*

His reservations about being involved in actual war turned out to be ironic since he was torpedoed and died in the second month of World War 1.

Engine Room Conditions

*We were according to programme due back in Malta on the 2ⁿᵈ of August but on the morning of the 28ᵗʰ July we received orders to get under weigh immediately and proceed at full speed to Port Said. We were in two watches part of the time and the heat in the engine rooms and stokeholds was simply awful and I am sure if we went to war for a lengthy period some better ventilating arrangements would have to be adopted or else there would be no need for wasting gunpowder as we would all be dead for want of air and food. I didn't enjoy the full power trial a little bit and on Sunday morning I had to turn and work on a very hot job. About 11.30 a.m. I resolved that I would be as well dead and with this intention I returned my lamp and scraper and sat down in a corner to await the end. While waiting someone told me that the rum was up. I reasoned with myself that I might just as well have my tot as leave it behind. I had it. Ah! This was better; much better. I changed my mind about dying and felt so elated that I made up my mind to go to the canteen in the evening and have some beer.*

Drinking on Shore Leave

*Monday the 1ˢᵗ of January 1912 was observed as a half holiday and being quarterly settlement day and plenty of money available, a goodly number of the boys made up for a quiet Xmas by a hilarious New Year (I am included in this lot). My mind was a blank from the 1ˢᵗ to the 4ᵗʰ but the usual "Rip and Tear" on Thursday afternoon (when I tested mess-stool and found same correct) brought me back to a sense of my responsibilities as a repeller of the German Invasion, and a great sobering effect was the result. It was too late in the year to make the annual resolutions or else I might have entertained thoughts about signing the pledge, etc.*

*Torquay is a beautifully situated town and is the mecca of the middle class who flock there to recuperate for a month or two after their arduous labours. I had not been ashore for some time and felt quite out of my element when I stepped on the macadamised highway. However I soon got used to it and finding I had almost forgotten the taste of liquor I resolved to fill up my bunkers to the brim as it might be the last leave granted in England for all I knew. I found a shop where the whisky was good and after a few samplers I settled to it in earnest. (My companions had gone off after a bit of something else so I was free to follow my own devices.) I stayed where I had anchored until 11 o'clock and then returned with the help of a gentleman whom I had picked up during the evening to the hotel where I had booked a bed. He told me he was a music-hall manager from Manchester and he left me near my hotel vowing eternal friendship and I, not to be outdone in matters of felicitation, promptly fell on his neck; in token of friendship which nearly ended in disaster. I turned to enter my hotel and was rather surprised to find it going round and round at a terrifying speed and bumped myself rather heavily when stepping through what I took to be the door. I made one or two unsuccessful attempts to enter and then sailor-like I changed my tactics and, by carefully finding the speed at which the place was revolving and waiting until the door was nearly opposite, I side-stepped quickly, and with a Ho! Heave! Ho! and a breast stroke I was inside and holding on to the mat for all I knew. My mode of entry soon brought the landlord on the scene and knowing I was in capable hands I resigned myself to his charge and any subsequent events failed to interest me.*

*I awoke next morning with my head much too large for my cap, swelled I expect where I had bumped it the previous evening, and a thirst that was honestly worth a quid. I had a few gin and gingers to cool my parched tongue and made a resolution to be a teetotaler for the future; which resolution was promptly broken at seven bells when they served out the rum.*

## RELIGION AND POLITICS

*If the Maltese are not robbed by capitalism they are under the thumb of oppressors equally as powerful. I refer to the priests of the Roman Catholic religion. It is a well known fact that wherever you find Roman Catholicism in a flourishing condition, just as certain are you to find the masses in poverty and ignorance. They have splendid churches in Malta but on their steps you find the beggar in his worst aspect. What will God think of a people who build splendid churches to his memory and neglect the broken images on the marble steps? Somewhere in the good book it says, "If you have neglected one of those you have also forgotten me."*

*It is unnecessary however to go to Malta to see broken images. There are thousands of them in England. I have seen many. I have studied the crowd on the embankment after midnight. I have seen the unemployed and the hunger marchers. I have been in some of our workhouses as a visitor. I have seen prostitutes plying for hire, endeavouring to earn a livelihood, selling their soul for a piece of silver under the shadow of a church; girls working sixteen hours a day in miserable attics in the East End. Making fancy blouses and finery for ladies' hats and earning about five shillings a week. I believe that on many of the gorgeous robes and gee-gaw finery displayed on the backs of the noble wearers at some of the West End balls and parties are tears dropped by those poor seamstresses.*

*What is wrong? What will God think of Christian England where people make necklaces and plumes for hats and fancy blouses for the aristocrats before they make bread for themselves? Eighty thousand children in London alone go to school every day badly clothed and hungry. Is it humane to try and cram knowledge into their poor little heads when their stomachs are empty? I have seen those poor children marched round the playground, with their toes sticking through their boots on Empire day, carrying union jacks made in Germany and singing some doggerel concocted by Roseberry about the glorious flag and the Empire on which the sun never sets. I am glad some of the teachers have made a stand against this hollow sham and voiced their opinions in no uncertain voice. Those same teachers at the conference held at Plymouth have struck out against the sharp line drawn between the curriculum for the secondary school and the one for the schools of the working class. They even went so far as to say that the curriculum drawn up for the children of the workers was intended to keep them what the upper classes want them to be, namely, hewers of wood and drawers of water.*

*There is however in England a cloud on the horizon; a cloud as yet no bigger than a man's hand but one that threatens in the near future to spread across the civilized countries of the world and bind them together in the holy bounds of brotherhood and love. The golden cloud of socialism. "Socialism" as Lord Roseberry said in his great Glasgow speech to the merchants and magnates of that city, "is the end of all things". True words Roseberry. The end of a good many things for you, probably a reduction in the number of racing stables and kennels where horses and dogs are better housed and fed than many of the working classes who produce your rent and profits.*

182

*"Socialism is the child of the devil" said a well known clergyman a few months ago. The church has always sided with the strongest party, has invariably helped the strong against the weak; the rich against the poor, and until there are real signs that the people are in earnest about possessing their own, then, and not till then will the church take any sort of a decided stand. I have often pondered on the position of the church today and thought to myself that it is fast being driven into a false position by modern capitalism. Christianity was a movement engineered and promulgated by poor working men. All great and lasting movements have come from the same source.*

*There is a General Election in Britain just now and it is decidedly amusing to stand afar off and listen to the echoes of the battle cries that reach us. In Britain a shibboleth, a mere phrase, is often as formidable as an army. Take for instance a phrase in common use at this time; "Grandmotherly Legislation"! It is only a cheap sneer. It means nothing, proves nothing, leads no whither; but it is accepted by millions of our hard practical minds as a sufficient answer to any suggestion that a government ought really to govern. Suggest that a nation should feed and teach the children, or that the nation should not let a man, who is a wealth producing machine, stand idle and eat his head off, and the silly old phrase is brought out to knock you down with, you are accused of grandmotherly legislation: and your hard-headed, practical countrymen shrug their shoulders and go on their practical way.*

*Well, let us take this phrase by the nose and see what it is good for. Let us take one example of our grandmotherly incapacity for legislation and consider it as hardheaded and practical men should consider things. Let us take the problem*

183

of unemployment. We have as a rule close on one million unemployed. These men beg, or steal, or starve, or become paupers, or loafers or tramps. Any attempt to employ them would be called "grandmotherly legislation". And we hard-headed, practical men are so afraid of that phrase that we do - nothing. It if would be "grandmotherly legislation" to find hungry men work, or to give hungry children food and love, what is it to let them starve, or rot or go to the devil? It is what we call hard-headed practical sense. Such a funny name to give it. But we are a funny people. Here is an unemployed man. He is a shoemaker, let us say. Why is he unemployed? There is no work for him. Have we then, too many shoes? Obviously, or he would be asked to make more. I see: but - look at the feet of the people in the street. They are not well shod, many of them. And there are children not shod at all. Only a few days ago a London school teacher said that many of her scholars came barefooted to school in winter. Too many boots? That cannot be the answer.

If you go to one of the gifted and cultured leaders of the hardheaded and ask him why the shoemaker is out of work he will quack most learnedly about the law of supply and demand. The law of my eye and Betty Martin. The law of stuff and nonsense. Only a hardheaded, practical Britisher could tolerate such pedantic twaddle. Did you ever hear of a horse being left out of work by the law of supply and demand? Did you ever see a horse tramping the roads or sleeping under hedges without an owner? Now, there is a suggestive word; owner. But a man has no owner; nobody owns him. The children go to school with bare feet; the shoemaker starves for want of work. It is all quite practical and we are saved from the "grandmotherly legislation" which would find shoes for the children and work for the man.

My own political views were honed in South Africa during the era of apartheid. I grew up in a liberal South African household; my parents entertained black guests at a time when such contacts across the colour bar were rare. It was ironic, however, that our African servants were surly about serving meals to guests they regarded as no different from themselves. When I was eleven the Nationalist government came to power and apartheid intensified. Racial discrimination had been a fact of life for many years; our servants had to carry passes after the evening curfew so that they could legally walk through the "white" areas of the town to their families in the black "location" or township on the outskirts. Occasionally I would be asked to write out a pass after my parents had gone out for the evening. In 1948 the government began to pass legislation under the guise of "separate development" which would strip away the few rights Africans, Indians and Coloureds had. My father became heavily involved in the campaign against the government's proposals to close the open universities to blacks and I remember his speeches being reported in the local press and him marching in protest with faculty and students down the main street of our town in full academic dress. Later when I was a student I did the same over further discriminatory legislation. I became a supporter first of the so-called "radical" Liberal Party and then of the African National Congress. As a graduate student and then a university teacher in England I worked as a volunteer for the Anti-Apartheid Movement and for the election of Harold Wilson and the Labour Party in 1964. So grandfather's heartfelt diatribes against the ravages caused by capitalism and religious bigotry strike a chord in me. His views on socialism, on class structure and on prostitution are far-sighted and perceptive.

# CHAPTER 10: THE SINKING OF HMS PATHFINDER

The Mediterranean voyage of HMS Lancaster ended in November, 1912 after a commission lasting two years and six months. James McKay's service record indicates that he was attached to the naval barracks named HMS Pembroke in Chatham from then until April 1914. He was seconded during this time to be Inspector of Works at Fairfield Shipbuilding and Engineering Company on the banks of the River Clyde in Glasgow. They were a major builder of warships for the Royal Navy and other navies before and during both World Wars. Interestingly they constructed a number of the "Empress" transatlantic passenger liners for Canadian Pacific. Although his record does not indicate exactly what his duties at the shipyard were, naval officers acted as consultants during the building of a warship. From April, 1914 he was once more training engine room personnel until he was called up in July to serve on the cruiser HMS Pathfinder. On the 1st of June in 1914 he had been promoted from Engine Room Artificer to Artificer Engineer.

The First World War broke out in August, 1914. Pathfinder was patrolling the entrance to the Firth of Forth to protect the naval base of Rosyth situated inside the Firth. In order to conserve her supplies of coal she was forced to limit her speed to 6 knots, a factor which became crucial in her first taste of active warfare. The German submarine U21, commanded by Kapitan-Leutnant Otto Hersing, was one of a flotilla stationed at Heligoland in the North Sea anticipating an attack by ships of the Royal Navy. However the British fleet stayed safely at home in port and did not venture out. On August the 8th, U21 and the submarine flotilla were sent out on patrol to intercept British warships escorting troop convoys to France. The patrol was forced back to base by heavy weather. A second patrol was also curtailed by weather but finally U21 made the 800 kilometer voyage across the North Sea to the east coast of Scotland. She ventured inside the Firth but submerged and beat a hasty retreat when she was spotted and fired on. A day or so later Otto Hersing finally found his prey. Here is the account of how he stalked Pathfinder from his book about his war service published in 1932:

## Firing the first torpedo of the war and the first in history

*5 September 1914*

*A glorious autumn day; the sea a mirror of greenish grey. On the shore, shrouded in smoke, the outline of suburban houses; one sensed the intense movement of a port: Edinburgh. U21 had been stationed for a whole day in the Firth of Forth.*

*Nothing.*

*Not a single boat raised its anchor or returned to port. The long, useless wait got on the crew's nerves and niggled my pride as the submarine commander. Where was the offensive efficacy of our submarine fleet going to end up? Had one of our submarines already had the chance of firing its torpedoes? The long wait was putting our pride as submariners to a difficult test .... A coastguard vessel approached, raising a white moustache of foam: we could make out the funnel....*

*At last! Smoke on the horizon; thick, black smoke. Much more promising. I clutched my telescope. Possible prey? It was an enemy cruiser; we recognized it by its mast and funnels. A rapid rush of thoughts, a quick assessment of probabilities: Should I abandon my safe position near the port and try an attack from some distance? It would be a problem. Suddenly I remembered that it was Saturday. The weekend. The British don't spend their weekend on the high seas. They enjoy it much more spending it in port. Even so, even in wartime, I was sure, absolutely sure, that the English would eventually arrive without making us wait for long. I had only to make towards their route.*

*The hours passed in a slow eternity.... And if they didn't come? In that case, the commanders of the torpedo boats and cruisers would have an ironic laugh and, in the mess, with glasses of wine in hand, they would exchange their views: 'As our Admiral Tirpitz said so well, a submarine is a plaything for peacetime'. The cruiser had disappeared. Not even a trace of smoke on the horizon. Then, suddenly, there they were: the masts... a funnel.... the cruiser was approaching us directly and without deviating. The whole crew was electrified, as though charged up by a battery. Hearts beat faster, brains in a fever. The enemy was approaching. It was right in front of us, clearly visible, in the best position for being attacked. It was the moment to react. We had to react.*

*I glanced at the clock. It was exactly four o'clock when I made my preparations. The target was coming closer, ever closer.... What was about to be fired was the first torpedo of our war. No one could know what consequences the enormous explosives contained in the torpedo might have on the submarine itself at such range. Would U21 be able to*

189

*tolerate it?  Would the flotation tanks and the fuel tanks be squashed?  Above all, what would happen to the storage batteries?*

*However, I did not indulge myself for long in these thoughts.  I wanted to maneuver myself into the best position for the shot and fire my torpedo.  What might then happen was a secondary issue which ought not to distract me at all at this moment.  I wanted to load both the firing tubes and launch both my torpedoes so that if one did not reach its target, or did not fire, at least the other would have a chance.  The helmsman, Gedan, who was at my side in the conning tower turned to me and said: "Captain, for this cruiser we only need one torpedo which will certainly hit its target.  Our torpedoes are excellent and in peace time you, Captain, were the best torpedoist in the whole navy."  That man knew how to touch my ambition: I had only one firing tube loaded.*

*We prepared ourselves for the attack.  U21 was highly maneuverable when submerged.  Everyone awaited the command to fire with bated breath.  The cruiser came ever closer; it was soon in our sights: it was exactly 4.45 when I pressed the electric button. The torpedo, driven by compressed air, exited from the tube and made for the target.  I immediately lowered the periscope so as not to give my presence away to the enemy.  Now we, enclosed in our steel tomb, waited.  Had the torpedo reached its target?  If so, would the submarine survive?  Would it disintegrate following the explosion of such an enormous quantity of material in our immediate vicinity?*

*The seconds passed, with all the speed of drops of syrup falling.*

*Ten seconds.. nothing.*

190

*Twenty.*

*Thirty.... Damn! By now it should have....*

*Nothing happened, absolutely nothing.*

*Half a minute had already passed. The torpedo should have reached the ship long ago. One minute. The torpedo must have passed without hitting. We were completely downcast. The last vestige of hope had fallen, like the last grain of sand in an hourglass. But how could it have happened? How? I was certain I had manoeuvred with the utmost precision.*

*I looked at the clock. 1 minute and 15 seconds had passed since the shot was fired. The torpedo had not found its mark. Some unforeseen incident had supervened....Suddenly, it seemed the whole world was collapsing. A terrifying detonation reverberated and a cosmic force shook the submarine. My first thought, as soon as I could regain self-control, was: 'Has the hull managed to resist?' And I shouted: 'Reports!'*

*'Everything is in order!'*

*Thanks be to God.*

*The storage battery? Also in order.*

*Everything had gone well. Now I could trust myself to look at the effect of the terrifying explosion on the enemy. I raised the periscope. Of the cruiser, not a trace was left. According to British reports, I found out later that I had hit the cruiser in the centre where, between the funnels, a powder magazine had exploded. The front funnel, blown into the air,* *had fallen far away in the sea. The cruiser had split in two: the front section sank bow first, immediately. The stern section rose up, floated for a while and then sank more slowly. Of the entire crew, 350 men strong, only 11 sailors were saved by a torpedo boat and by British coastguards who rushed to the spot. My victim was the British cruiser 'Pathfinder' which was utterly destroyed in three and a half minutes on the 5<sup>th</sup> September, 1914. This happened thanks to the first torpedo ever launched by a submarine. It was also the first time in world history that a warship had become the victim of a torpedo.*

On the evening after the sinking, the Secretary of the Admiralty announced to the press that: "HMS Pathfinder (Captain Francis Martin Leake) struck a mine today at 4.30 p.m. about twenty miles off the East Coast and foundered very rapidly. The loss of life has probably been heavy." The Admiralty concealed the fact that submarines had penetrated British defenses and that Pathfinder had been torpedoed, not mined. The following day a further communiqué stated that: "…it transpires that about 90 of the crew, dead and wounded, were picked up by torpedo boats and taken to a base hospital. Captain Leake, who commanded the vessel, and other officers have also been saved." James McKay was amongst the officers listed as missing in the next communiqué issued two days after the sinking. On Tuesday the 8<sup>th</sup> of September the names of casualties among the crew were added to the list of officers' names making a total of 269, of which 5 were listed as dead, 15 wounded and 249 missing. By Friday, under pressure from press reports containing eye witness accounts and questions in the House of Commons, the Admiralty lifted its censorship and revealed that a torpedo fired from a U-boat caused the disaster. 232 men were listed as dead, including my grandfather.

The nearest witness to the tragedy was the lookout on board a trawler about three and a half miles away. He told the press that it happened on a lovely day with a calm sea. He recognized the Pathfinder as a British ship as he had seen her on patrol before. She was about 10 miles from the shore and not going very fast when he felt his boat being violently shaken from end to end. The skipper had immediately rushed up on deck and together they saw a great cloud of smoke and steam rise up "just like a big white mountain and it rose and rose until at the end you would have thought it was just an ordinary cloud." When it cleared he could see the stern sticking straight up out of the water. "It slipped slowly down and then disappeared with a great rush. The whole thing hadn't lasted three minutes from the time I had been admiring her until she sank from sight." He then saw the two torpedo boats rushing for the site followed by two more. They were soon picking up people. By the time their trawler and various other boats arrived on the scene there were no bodies to be seen; nothing but wreckage littering the sea for about a mile around: splinters, clothes and a piece of a small boat with Pathfinder written on it. Gradually more wreckage surfaced; he saw shattered pieces of the ship and the mast. "It must have been a terrible explosion; I don't want to see the likes of yon again, I tell you."

On Wednesday the 9th of September The Scotsman published an interview with one of the survivors rescued from the water. He said that the sailors were going about their normal routines when the sudden crash came, which made the vessel shudder from end to end "like the quiver of some mammoth creature in agony." They were knocked down by

193

the explosion and, when he struggled to his knees, all was dark with wreckage of all kinds falling around out of the smoke. He ran aft and, on the orders of the officers, helped throw overboard anything which might help survivors float: brooms, oars, lumps of wood and gratings. He emphasized that there was no panic even though most of the lifeboats were too badly damaged to be launched. When the order "Every man for himself" was given they took to the water and clung to wreckage. One petty officer and a lieutenant who were strong swimmers swam from man to man assisting them with wooden pieces of wreckage. While they waited for help the petty officer encouraged them to join in the singing of "Tipperary" and other more bawdy ballads to keep up their morale. Some slipped away from their supports down into the sea and disappeared. A cheer went up when the remaining survivors spotted the torpedo boats racing toward them.

An account of the sinking was written at the time by Lieutenant-Commander E.O. Stallybrass, who was an officer aboard HMS Pathfinder, but not published in The Naval Review until April. 1971:

"At about 3.50 p.m. we were disturbed at tea by an almighty crash. The torpedo had hit our starboard side under the bridge, and the explosion had touched off the fore magazine. The crash was followed by a breathless silence, and after some seconds (it seemed) the crockery in the pantry fell to the deck, the lights went out and the deck seemed to shudder under our feet. A large piece of timber came down through the quarter-deck skylight and broke the table, spilling tea over my trousers."

He rushed up on deck with other officers and threw wooden gear over the side to provide buoyancy for survivors

194

in the water. The three ship's boats were smashed; the fourth was badly damaged but served as buoyancy for 14 survivors. The captain ordered a shot to be fired to warn the base at May Island of their predicament. The bow of the ship he describes as being well down in the water with most of it forward of the bridge having been blown off. Since most of the crew below was at tea he assumes that they would have been killed instantly by the blast. About five minutes after the ship was hit she suddenly lurched forward to 40 degrees and soon the water was swirling around their feet. "The captain said 'Jump, you devils, jump.' All except two of us jumped. The captain stayed with his ship until she sank, and Bath (his secretary) stopped to unlace his boots. Both were saved......I was carried away from the ship by the swirl in the water...... I was fully dressed so I started undressing. Wellingtons came off easily enough, but I had an awful struggle with the monkey jacket; eventually I put my hands over my head and sank out of it, but it's a very clumsy method. I was glad to get my collar off – it had started to shrink and was choking me."

He looked back at the ship and saw the stern at an angle of about 60 degrees before it sank, slowly at first and then with a rush. He estimated that from the first explosion to the sinking had taken about 15 minutes and that he had been in the water for about 10 minutes. He found a bunch of life jackets and tossed them to others. After about an hour he was picked up by one of the torpedo boats.

In 1942 he added to this account by reconstructing from memory what had happened before and after the torpedo struck the ship. The track of the torpedo had been spotted by the Chief Boatswain's Mate who called out to the officer on the watch. If Pathfinder had been steaming at or near her maximum speed of 25 knots or even at 15 knots - which was the minimum speed set for warships in the vicinity of enemy submarines - she could have reduced the chances of being hit by using the rudder to turn and face it. However Stallybrass states that: "at full speed she burned an excessive amount of coal, her bunker capacity was small and, in order to maintain her patrol for five days a week and have full speed available at ten minutes' notice, she could only steam at six knots while on patrol." This was not fast enough for the rudder to be effective. The Officer of the Watch attempted to take evasive action by ordering starboard engine full astern and port full ahead. Stallybrass remembered the Senior Engineer saying that the starboard engine was put astern but that the working of the port telegraph gave the impression that the operator completely lost his head and did not respond to the order.

Stallybrass is suggesting that the ship might have avoided the torpedo had the operator complied with the orders from the bridge. A number of naval histories written in the past twenty years contain accounts of the Pathfinder disaster; all repeat the conclusions reached by Stallybrass that the engine room was to blame. Brayton Harris and Richard Compton Hall refer to an incredulous throttle man not obeying the telegraph orders. Yet two accounts from histories of the Great War dated 1914 and 1918 make no mention of this neglect of orders. It is clear that the later accounts are based on the Stallybrass article, especially that written by Compton Hall which repeats his phrases almost verbatim.

I must acknowledge that I am defensive of the engine room crew because my grandfather was one of them and may well have been the operator at the throttle as that was one of the duties of an Artificer Engineer. Grandfather relates several experiences he had with incompetence among the officers he encountered so I was dubious about this particular officer's conclusions reached in his reconstruction of events 28 years after they had taken place. I was curious about whether a Court of Enquiry had been set up to investigate negligence as had been the case in the sinking by the German submarine U-9 of three British cruisers 17 days later. In that case the court found errors of judgment by the Captain of the first ship torpedoed. If the Admiralty had suspicions that the loss of Pathfinder and of 232 of her officers and men could have been averted had orders been obeyed surely they would have set up an enquiry?

I spent two full days in the British National Archives in London tracking down all the documents I could find relating to Pathfinder. My search was like a scavenger hunt where a clue in one document led to a reference to another which could only be tracked with the help of a staff member. In all, I had the resources of four specialists who were familiar with the ins and outs of the section related to naval documents. Once I had been given a reference number I had to call it up on a computer so that it could be searched out and delivered to a locker marked with my seat number. Two of the "documents" turned out to be immense volumes measuring about four feet by three feet and weighing so much that I was given a trolley to transport them to a table one at a time. These contained indexed entries written in pen and ink in a beautiful copperplate hand. One entry covering Pathfinder simply read: "Court of Enquiry cancelled. Captain Leake's Report." Adjacent to it was a number – X 3626. With the help of assistants who tracked down the reference I found the full record relating to the sinking. It consisted of various reports and copies of correspondence between the Admiral commanding the coast of Scotland and the Secretary of the Admiralty in London. All the documents were marked secret. The first was the Admiral's report on the loss dated the 6th of

September – the day following the sinking. He had interviewed a number of the survivors and had heard from Captain Leake who was suffering from injuries and shock. All confirmed that the ship had been torpedoed by a submarine. He stated that the Chief Boatswain's mate had spotted a periscope 3000 yards off the starboard bow shortly before seeing the track of the torpedo and raised the alarm to the bridge. His report goes on to say that Engineer Lieutenant Evington told him (the Admiral) that the orders given to the port engine "could not have had sufficient time to take effect on the movements of the ship." I was delighted to find this clear vindication of the engine room crew.

Captain Leake had forwarded his report on the loss to the Admiral from the Hospital Yacht "Sheelah" where he had been recovering from his wounds; this was included with the Admiral's documents I found. He was not on the bridge at the time the torpedo struck but stated: "I heard the screws easing down as if preparatory to some new engine orders. I moved to go on deck to ascertain the cause of this occurrence and, simultaneously, the ship gave a veritable stagger which lasted for some seconds and caused all movable gear to fall and hatch covers to close." Once he got to the quarter-deck with debris raining down around him he found the First Lieutenant and three Petty Officers in charge of crew members working to throw floating objects overboard and to allay panic, of which he said, there was no sign. Attempts were made to launch the small boats but they were too badly damaged. He was last to leave the ship. After he landed up in the water he encountered an Able Seaman who told him he had been on the bridge at the time of the explosion and that the Officer of the Watch had put the helm over and altered the telegraphs before the torpedo struck. Captain Leake noted that he did not at any time hear any complaints or panic, nor did he see incidents that were not correct behaviour. Again his report makes no mention of the engine room failing to comply with the orders given by the telegraphs. In fact what brought the captain on deck just before the ship was hit was a change in the sound of the propellers, suggesting that the throttle man did respond to the order but that it came with insufficient time to take effect, as the Chief Engineer Lieutenant stated in his interview with the Admiral.

On receipt of the Admiral's report the Secretary of the Admiralty directed him to set up a Court of Enquiry to "elucidate the circumstances attending this disaster as soon as Captain Leake had recovered sufficiently to give evidence." Three days later the Admiral wrote back from Scotland giving reasons why an enquiry should not be held. He reported that all the survivors except for Captain Leake and a few wounded men in hospital had been sent on leave in accordance with Admiralty policy in cases of disaster. It would therefore be difficult to reassemble the crew. Furthermore the Admiral believed that his interviews with key survivors and the report by Captain Leake himself provided sufficient detail of the circumstances surrounding the loss. The Admiralty cancelled the Court of Enquiry. Would they have done so had there been a suspicion of negligence on the part of the engine room? I believe not. In fact the entire crew was commended by the Admiralty for "exemplary steadiness and coolness" and the excellent discipline which prevailed, "every order being promptly obeyed without the slightest confusion." The message concludes: "My Lords desire that an expression of their satisfaction and appreciation may be conveyed to the officers and men concerned." This is in sharp contrast to the accounts by Stallybrass and his followers about confusion in the engine room and an incredulous throttle man's failure to follow orders because he had completely lost his head.

# EPILOGUE

My grandfather's voyage ended with his death on board HMS Pathfinder. The wreck which is his tomb lies 16 miles from St Abb's Head off the west coast of Scotland. It was located by Clive Cussler and his marine survey team in 1984. The Admiralty has placed an embargo on divers exploring the ship since it is the graveyard of so many men who went down with her. Curiously enough Cussler also located the wreck of U-21, which lies off the east coast of Northern England some 600 kms away. At the end of the war the Royal Navy ordered her to sail from Kiel to the naval base at Harwich. Rather than have her suffer the ignominy of falling into enemy hands, Captain Otto Hersing and his crew scuttled the submarine. They were rescued from the sea and were eventually repatriated to Germany.

My journey with my grandfather ended with my research into the Admiralty archives. I began the journey with the intention of following the itinerary described in his diary to explore the places around the Mediterranean one hundred years after he had done so. It soon evolved into a deeper and more meaningful quest: to know and, ultimately, to love this shadowy presence from my past. Love may seem a strong word. Yet it is not meant in a sentimental way for I believe love is an active verb rather than an abstract noun. Grandfather gave me a number of gifts. Through his elegant style of writing he taught me to write more clearly and to attempt to describe what I saw and heard more vividly. I found myself in sympathy with his feelings about the navy and especially the snobbishness of the officers and the tyranny of the naval hierarchy. His outspoken radical views on the church and on politics struck a chord in me. His advocacy of socialism was admirable and of their time, idealistic and untainted by the excesses of later years in many countries. I also admired his devotion to the well-being of his young family exemplified by his joining the navy to support them when other career options were closed to him. This took courage because he had negative feelings towards ships and to the sea.

His travels gave me a purpose beyond being simply a gawping tourist in the cities and towns of the Mediterranean that he described. Travelling with this sense of purpose was a gift, in that he gave me many examples of how to cast a careful eye over local cultures and their peoples with the same warm appreciation that his diary displays. At times throughout the narrative he makes an appearance as a protective guardian whose presence I valued and almost sensed directly. Various life lessons helped further my growth as a human being too. The love between us culminated in my discovery through frustrating hours of research that he and his colleagues in the engine room of HMS Pathfinder had been wrongfully held responsible for the sinking of the ship. This was the ultimate vindication which I trust will challenge the erroneous views put forward in various histories of the Royal Navy.

Made in the USA
Charleston, SC
06 October 2014